Container Gardening FOR DUMMIES®

PORTABLE EDITION

**by Bill Marken
& the Editors of The National
Gardening Association**

D0090024

WILEY

Wiley Publishing, Inc.

Container Gardening For Dummies®, Portable Edition

Published by
Wiley Publishing, Inc.
111 River St.
Hoboken, NJ 07030-5774
www.wiley.com

Copyright © 2006 by Wiley Publishing, Inc., Indianapolis, Indiana

Published by Wiley Publishing, Inc., Indianapolis, Indiana

Published simultaneously in Canada

For general information on our other products and services, please contact our Customer Care Department within the U.S. at 800-762-2974, outside the U.S. at 317-572-3993, or fax 317-572-4002.

For technical support, please visit www.wiley.com/techsupport.

Wiley also publishes its books in a variety of electronic formats. Some content that appears in print may not be available in electronic books.

Library of Congress Control Number: 2006922228

ISBN-13: 978-0-470-04370-7

ISBN-10: 0-470-04370-9

Manufactured in the United States of America

10 9 8 7 6 5 4 3 2 1

1B/QR/QT/QW/IN

WILEY

About the Authors

Bill Marken is an editor and writer in the San Francisco Bay Area. He was editor-in-chief of *Sunset, the Magazine of Western Living,* from 1981 to 1996. While at *Sunset,* he wrote for the garden section, worked on editions of the *Western Garden Book,* and nurtured his interests in gardening, landscaping, and travel. He developed an early interest in gardening by working at nurseries while going to school; he may have been the only English major at U. C. Berkeley who knew what U.C. soil mix was.

The National Gardening Association is the largest member-based, nonprofit organization of home gardeners in the U.S. Founded in 1972 to spearhead the community garden movement, today's National Gardening Association is best known for its bimonthly publication, *National Gardening* magazine. Reporting on all aspects of home gardening, each issue is read by some half-million gardeners worldwide. These publishing activities are supplemented by online efforts, such as on the World Wide Web (www.garden.org).

Dedication

To Mike MacCaskey of the National Gardening Association, who told me enough about the plans for this book to get me excited but not enough to persuade me to do something more sensible. Thanks, too, for pitching in all along the way.

Author's Acknowledgments

Special thanks go to Lance Walheim, Peggy Henry, Martha Polk Wingate, Nan Sterman, Emily Stetson, Catherine Boyle, David Els, Michael MacCaskey, Larry Sommers, Charlie Nardozzi, Suzanne DeJohn, and Kathy Bond-Bori.

Publisher's Acknowledgments

We're proud of this book; please send us your comments through our Dummies online registration form located at www.dummies.com/register/.

Some of the people who helped bring this book to market include the following:

Acquisitions, Editorial, and Media Development

Editor: Corbin Collins

(Previous Edition: Tim Gallan)

Editorial Program Assistant: Courtney Allen

Editorial Supervisor and Reprint Editor: Carmen Krikorian

Editorial Manager: Michelle Hacker

Editorial Program Coordinator: Hanna Scott

Editorial Assistants: Nadine Bell, David Lutton

Cover Photo: © Brand X Pictures

Cartoons: Rich Tennant (www.the5thwave.com)

Composition Services

Project Coordinator: Kristie Rees

Layout and Graphics: Jonell Burns, Joyce Haughey, Kathie Rickard, Brent Savage

Proofreader: Laura Albert

Indexer: Sherry Massey

Illustrator: Mark Zahnd

Publishing and Editorial for Consumer Dummies

Diane Graves Steele, Vice President and Publisher, Consumer Dummies

Joyce Pepple, Acquisitions Director, Consumer Dummies

Kristin A. Cocks, Product Development Director, Consumer Dummies

Kathleen Nebenhaus, Vice President and Executive Publisher, Consumer Dummies, Lifestyles, Pets, Education

Publishing for Technology Dummies

Andy Cummings, Vice President and Publisher, Dummies Technology/General User

Composition Services

Gerry Fahey, Vice President of Production Services

Debbie Stailey, Director of Composition Services

Contents at a Glance

Table of Contents

Introduction

··

*L*ook up *container gardening* in a reference book and you may find out that the ancient Romans grew laurel (for their wreaths) in marble urns, or that Moses carried a pot-full of rushes with him everywhere on his long travels. Fair enough. But the real origin of growing plants in containers as we know it today goes back to southern California, specifically Pasadena in the early 1950s, I seem to recall hearing, when a man sitting by a kidney-shaped swimming pool thought, "Wouldn't it be even nicer if I could reach over to a handy, fragrantly-blooming tree and pick a lemon to squeeze in my drink?"

The good life in the garden is what growing plants in containers is about. You don't grow container plants to put food on the table — but as you'll find out later, some container-grown tomatoes may be nice in a salad. You don't grow container plants to prevent erosion or even to keep your front yard green and mud-free so that your lawn-proud neighbors won't gripe. You grow plants in containers for fun.

In this book, we want to share with you the many pleasures of container plants. The fun comes in discovering the amazing number of plant possibilities and the equally amazing variety of containers. You can get immense satisfaction from growing something beautiful, in creating interesting combinations of plants, in experimenting with new plants, in getting to know plants much more intimately than you can know the same plants in the ground.

But what about all the work involved, you say? We'll be talking about that too: how to plant, how to water, how to feed, how to repot, and all that. And we should also mention that stuff isn't work if you enjoy growing container plants — which you will.

How to Use This Book

You can use this book very successfully if you have never grown a plant before. If that's you, better read the first two chapters first to get a sense of what's involved in growing container plants and what your climate and garden will allow and encourage.

Whatever level your gardening skill happens to be, feel free to skip around and look for ideas when you need them. If you want ideas on plants to try, check out Chapters 6 through 9. If you have your containers and plants all ready to go, better turn to Chapters 4 and 5 and start planting. If something is mysteriously afflicting your geraniums, turn to Chapter 12 right now.

What We Assume about You

We don't expect you to know much at all about gardening. As we mentioned, this book is useful for both novice and experienced gardeners. We expect that you enjoy growing plants and will do the work that's necessary to plant and maintain them.

Icons Used in This Book

 When we provide a tidbit of advice that will save you time, save you trouble, or help keep your plants healthy, we use this icon.

 This icon flags information that you ought to read carefully so that you retain it.

 We use this icon to indicate that what we're about to say will save your life, or at least the life of your plant.

Where to Go From Here

Turn to Chapter 1, take a look at the table of contents to see what topics catch your fancy, or look up something specific in the index.

The 5th Wave By Rich Tennant

"Aside from a little beginner's confusion, I've done very well with my bulbs."

Chapter 1

Neat Things to Do with Container Plants

*A*re you timid about growing plants in containers? What's more persuasive than the sight of a container full to the brim with spring's bounty of red tulips, the lip-smacking appeal of ripe strawberries dangling from a hanging basket, or the inspired zaniness of cactus rising from an old cowboy boot? Containers can provide a healthy, happy home for an array of indoor and outdoor greenery, and the attraction reaches beyond simply pairing a pot with a plant.

✔ Growing plants in pots, baskets, tubs, barrels, or other containers up to and including discarded footwear can be fun in a garden of any size and shape. If your gardening space consists of a small deck, a porch, or unfriendly soil or weather, container gardening may be your ticket to growing something green or colorful.

✔ Growing plants in pots is easy. Witness the neglected geranium outside the front door of your dry cleaner.

✔ Growing plants in pots can be as challenging as anything in gardening. Think of how much dedication and skill is involved in bonsai's pruning and pampering.

Whatever your skill level and garden situation, we want to help you match the right plants with the right containers and give them the kind of care that produces beautiful results.

Taking the Container Plunge?

Here we introduce some of the key concepts that run through this book — and offer at least four good reasons why you may choose to grow plants in containers.

1. You can grow plants in impossible places

Container plants are portable: They can grow where you don't have a conventional garden. Your chosen location may be a rooftop, a condominium deck, the porch of a mobile home, or a houseboat deck. Keep in mind how much water and light to provide, and all the other practical considerations that are covered later. And think about what purpose you want the container plants to serve. A spot of greenery? Some bright flowers? A privacy screen or hedge?

Even if you have only a tiny space available, you may want to picture your container plants as a "garden" with different plants complementing one another. For example, if you have room for only three plants, choose containers and plants of different sizes and styles; perhaps a 4-foot Japanese maple (lacy, fall color, leafless in winter), a 1-foot Mugho pine (mounding, evergreen), and a bowl of pansies in spring.

Or just move containers around in your own garden as the seasons change. In December, put a potted spruce on the front porch, and after the holidays, move it to the side of the house where it can bask in good light and water; put a pot of spring bulbs on the porch as the weather warms up.

2. You can make plants look good

Even if you have acres of gardens, you still may want a container plant or two. Highlighting a plant by growing it in a pot brings out qualities not noticeable in a garden bed. Notice how the containers enhance the plants in Figure 1-1. Take one of the most boring plants, Bar Harbor juniper, usually massed as a ground cover. Try planting a juniper in a rustic terra-cotta pot and see the instant transformation — the ordinary evergreen looks like a miniature weathered Sierra patriarch.

Figure 1-1: Various plants in various containers.

Maybe you prefer one special plant. Spoil it like an only child. Dote on a fussy but gorgeous azalea or a rare striped bamboo.

One pleasure of growing container plants is observing them up close. A 10-foot sunflower may look stunning against the back fence, but close-up viewing can be disappointing — what you see is several feet of bare stem. Better to grow something like a lace-cap hydrangea, whose intricate flower formations can absorb you on a summer day with a cool lemonade in hand.

3. You can grow plants that you think you can't grow

Containers allow and encourage experimentation. You can give plants the exact conditions that they need — which may be missing from your garden. You can provide the preferred soil mix, provide water in preferred doses, move plants around for best exposure (part shade for azaleas, full sun for cactus).

Containers let you grow plants with different soil and watering requirements side by side, not possible in a garden. Containers can be moved into protected spots during winter. Where are oranges growing in Minneapolis? In containers. Containers invite you to become friendly with certain plants — you discover what they like and don't like, what they respond to, and how they change during the seasons.

4. You can do stupid container tricks

What makes otherwise rational people grow living plants in all kinds of things? Old shoes, old toilets, old boats. Whatever the motivation, container gardeners can exercise spunk without polluting the atmosphere. Yes, some people may raise questions of taste, but an indiscretion or two is a small price to pay for fostering the creative spirit in all of us.

Remember the most important rule, which we describe in more detail later: Provide drainage.

An Out-of-Garden Experience

Before you take another step toward container gardening, make sure that you acknowledge and respect this concept: A container is not a natural place for a plant to grow.

A plant growing in the ground develops a network of roots to take in water and nutrients, gaining moisture from rain as well as your hose or sprinklers. If the plant gets too much sun or not enough, it clearly shows the effects with lanky growth, sunburned leaves, and, possibly, a painful death.

On the other hand, a container is confining, and without natural insulation, its contents dry out quickly. Nutrients wash out rapidly. The root system requires water and food in adequate doses. Roots run out of space and demand repotting. But think positively. You can improve the soil for a container far more dramatically than you can in the ground — your soil mix may not even contain actual soil (more on this in Chapter 4). Plus, if the plant doesn't respond well to its conditions, you may be able to move it to a spot it likes.

Container plants usually involve more time commitment than the same plants in the ground, but the rewards may exceed the investment.

What grows well in pots? Theoretically, just about anything for a while if the container is large enough. After all, nurseries sell giant sequoias in 5-gallon cans. But actually, not all plants are good candidates. Some look funny (corn keeps tipping over). Big shrubs and trees may look fine for a year or two. Some plants just take too long to reach their mature shapes and performance levels. Why grow a fruit tree (except a dwarf type) in a container? You can expect little more than a large green stick for the first few years.

Advantages of plants in pots

✔ You can give exactly the right soil the plant needs (sandy for cactus; high-acid for azaleas).

✔ You can move the plant around when weather doesn't suit it — into more or less shade or out of the cold.

✔ You can protect plants from pests. You're able to isolate them if you want to spray and use just the right control without having to worry about neighboring plants.

✔ You get to know them better. With container plants, you discover how to care for individual plants as they respond to your care.

Advantages of plants in the ground

✔ The soil provides a greater reservoir of water and food.

✔ More insulation for roots during hot or cold weather.

> ✔ Less maintenance generally is involved.
>
> ✔ Plants can grow to their full size and reach their highest level of performance (fruit or flowers, for instance).

Designing with Container Plants

Does the term "design" sound a bit pretentious for the container gardening process: picking plants to put in pots, mixing different plants in the same pots, or combining different pots — all to make things look as nice as possible? We're open to another word, but at least you can relate to what we're talking about. Bottom line: Your designs really depend on maintenance considerations — planning placement of plants, whether in the same container or in several containers grouped together, according to their shared requirements for care.

One plant in a container standing alone can be stunning — good news if that's all you have space for. But combining several or many container plants gives a greater effect — almost like a garden growing in the ground. Containers can do all the things that a whole garden can: announce the seasons, flash bright color, and create miniature slices of nature.

Thinking about style

Style issues can be especially perplexing because you aren't going to find any cut-and-dried rules — unlike, say, how deep to plant tulips. Here are a few general-direction reminders to keep in mind when creating container plantings:

> ✔ Work with what you already have. Use container plants to complement your home or garden. In an informal setting, for example, you may want to use tubs of mixed summer annuals. Cactus in shallow bowls lend a dramatic note to a contemporary setting.
>
> ✔ Think about color. Using mostly green or white creates a cooling effect. Bright hot colors (zinnias, for instance) heat things up.
>
> ✔ Consider the different shapes of the plants you're using — whether they're in individual containers, mixed plantings, or multiple containers. Start to think about the shapes of the plants that you're choosing and use them

to complement and contrast with each other. Sample shape categories include

- Tall spiky plants: snapdragons or New Zealand flax.
- Round mounded shapes: impatiens or lavender.
- Trailers: lobelia or ivy.

✔ Want formal or casual? Topiary is formal. So are symmetrical plants — picture two boxwoods in urns or tree roses lining a walk. Containers with same-color flowers are formal. Casual is mixed-color annuals and containers of different sizes, materials, and shapes.

✔ Repeat the same colors or plants. For example, use yellow marigolds in a cluster of pots near the beginning of a front walk and then again on the front porch.

✔ Scale is a big subject. Big spaces demand large containers, at least 20 or 24 inches in diameter. If you cluster pots, make sure to include at least one good-sized container with a taller plant in it.

Growing that one special plant

This book covers hundreds of plants — annuals, cactus, fruit trees, even eggplant — that can make special showings in individual pots. Presenting a star calls for one plant in one pot or several of the same type (four pansies, say) in one pot.

You always want to choose a container that's the right size for the plant (see Chapter 3 for advice on sizes).

As a general guideline for goods looks, the plant needs to be at least as tall as the container; this is particularly true of annuals. Put 12-inch-tall snapdragons in a pot that's at least 12 inches tall. Don't put 6-inch pansies in a 12-inch pot — their friendly faces may be overwhelmed by all that space.

Combining plants in containers

Mixed annuals, annuals with perennials, perennials with bulbs — plants can be combined in the same container in so many ways. Start with a dominant plant (Japanese maple, snapdragons, delphiniums) and add compatible mounding or trailing plants (lobelia, impatiens, and many others).

Making arrangements

Arranging groups of container plants is like hanging pictures or moving furniture — complete with possible backaches. Don't be afraid to move plants again and again. You're satisfying *your* taste. Container groupings generally look best with at least three plants; dozens can be accommodated.

A few basic rules apply for grouping container plants:

- ✔ Start by using matching types of containers, like terra-cotta, in different sizes. Make one or two pots a lot larger than the others. Throw in a maverick, like a glazed pot.

- ✔ For a big deck or expanse of paving, use lots of pots and mix sizes, styles, and shapes.

- ✔ Mix plants of different textures, colors, and heights. Think about the basic shape categories described earlier.

- ✔ Do just the opposite and group identical pots with identical plants. Nothing looks more smashing in spring than three 14-inch terra-cotta pots stuffed with red tulips.

- ✔ Raise some containers higher with bricks underneath or plant stands, adding emphasis and ease of viewing.

- ✔ Be careful with small plants: They tend to go unnoticed. Clumsy people trip on them (we know from experience).

- ✔ Try to place containers where people gather. A seating area, for instance, offers opportunity to view plants up close and appreciate their fragrance.

- ✔ In large gardens, place containers near the house where you can notice them. Container plants scattered selectively along garden paths can provide a pleasant surprise. Another good placement is in the transition zone between patio and lawn or between lawn and wild garden.

Putting It All Together

Here are some suggestions for growing and displaying container plants effectively in your garden:

✔ Put a single golden barrel cactus in a low 12-inch bowl. Slowly and magnificently, the cactus can fill the pot.

✔ Circle a small tree with eight or so terra-cotta containers overflowing with white impatiens. Plant eight impatiens seedlings in each 12-inch container.

✔ On a balcony, create a privacy screen with containers of bamboo or English laurel.

✔ By your front door, use a pair of topiary ivy balls in matching containers to greet visitors in a formal way.

✔ Announce spring with a window box full of sun-loving, early-blooming pansies and snapdragons.

✔ For the holidays, buy gallon-can-size spruce, pine, or other conifers, transplant them to terra-cotta or glazed pots, and decorate them with tiny glass balls for tabletop decorations. They'll do well indoors for a few weeks.

✔ If you live where Japanese maples thrive, there's nothing better for a striking container tree. For all-year good looks, choose colorful-leaf types (like Oshio Beni), or even colorful-bark varieties (such as Sango Kaku).

✔ Lead the way up front steps by flanking with big pots of white marguerites — one plant per each 14-inch pot.

✔ At the edge of a sunny patio overhead, hang baskets of bougainvillea — normally a vine, but a vivid-blooming trailer when allowed to free fall.

✔ On a blank shady wall, attach wire half-baskets — at least three, staggered at different heights — filled with blooming begonias, impatiens, and ferns for greenery.

Down-to-Earth Advice

Before you go to the nursery, a few nitty-gritty reminders:

✔ Containers can be messy. They may drip water and stain surfaces. Use saucers as described in Chapter 3.

✔ Patience is in order before annuals start blooming, when bulbs are drying out after bloom, and when deciduous shrubs are leafless. Consider a staging area where you can keep container plants when they're not at their best.

> ✔ Remember your climate and the limits it puts on plants, especially container plants. If you live in cold region, be prepared to move prized plants into protection when winter arrives. See the next chapter for more on climates.

One Last Thing: Plant Names

You'll see a lot of plant names in this book. Every plant has a two-part botanical name, identifying its genus and species. The botanical name always appears in italics with the genus name first and capitalized. For example, *Tagetes erecta* is the American marigold. The genus *(Tagetes)* refers to a group of closely related plants found in nature — all the marigolds. The species *(erecta)* refers to a specific member of the genus — the tall, orange-flowered American marigold.

Of course, most plants also have common names, but these can vary from place to place and time to time. *Nemophila menziesii* will always be the botanical name for the same plant, no matter where in the world you find it. But some people call it California bluebell, while others know it as baby blue eyes. To add to this confusion, different plants may share the same common name. For example, various kinds of butterfly flowers exist, in addition to butterfly bush and butterfly weed. Sometimes, the common name *is* the botanical name. For example, *Petunia hybrida*.

Some specialized plants have an additional name tacked on to their botanical names, indicating a *variety* (also called a clone or cultivar) that is much like the species but differing in some particular way, such as flower color. *Tagetes erecta* Snowbird is a white-flowered variety of the American marigold.

You can see why people who want to be precise stick to botanical names, but for most of us and for most of the time, common names work fine. And that's what we're going to use in this book. In case of confusion over a common name, check out the botanical name, usually given in parentheses.

Chapter 2

Cultivating Your Little Corner of the World

*W*hat can you grow in containers your little corner of the world? The answer isn't at all clear-cut. Bear with us: You can expect words like *factor*, *macro* or *micro*, and *local conditions* to sneak up in our discussion. That's because we're talking about what goes on with climate and nature and all their wondrous permutations and variabilities.

At the macro level, your choice in plants depends on your area's climate. Just as important are the microclimates in your own garden — sun, shade, and wind — and the limits and possibilities that they create for growing plants. To grow container plants really well, you need to consider both the macro and micro sides of things.

Portability expands the climate tolerance of container plants. You can bring them indoors for protection from the cold, move them into more sun if they're not getting enough, or move them to a shadier spot if they're sunburned. But life in a container also makes a plant more vulnerable to weather extremes. A container plant doesn't have the insulation against cold and heat as does the same plant in the ground.

Before you bring the joys of container gardening to your backyard, you need to figure out what kinds of plants your climate can support.

A Climate to Call Your Own

Although all kinds of conditions determine what plants can grow in a certain climate, cold — not heat or humidity — is usually the key consideration. All plants have a certain tolerance to cold temperatures. Below that temperature, a plant's tissues are damaged or destroyed; if cold temperatures are prolonged, the plant may die. A plant's ability to withstand a minimum temperature is called its *hardiness* (you say, for instance, that a fuchsia is *hardy* to 28°F). Individual plant hardiness can vary depending on growing conditions and climatic factors in addition to cold, but the hardiness numbers are the most useful figures we have.

The United States Department of Agriculture publishes useful maps showing plant hardiness zones. The zone boundaries are based on average winter minimum temperatures collected from 125,000 weather stations. North America is divided into 11 zones, the warmest (zone 11) having an average winter minimum temperature above 40°F. Each succeeding zone down to zone 1 averages 10 degrees colder. Zones 1 through 10 are further divided into "a" and "b" in order to distinguish zones where average winter minimum differ by 5°F.

Zone systems based on average minimum temperatures are also available for Western Europe, South Africa, Australia, New Zealand, Japan, and China.

Plants mentioned in this book are identified by climate zone according to the lowest winter temperatures that they can withstand. For example, a tree that is recommended as hardy for USDA zone 5 can be reliably grown in that zone and milder ones (higher numbers) — areas where temperatures do not fall below -20°F.

If you make comparisons between climates within the same USDA zones, you can see some of the weaknesses of the hardiness zone system. For example, zone 9 is in both Florida and California. Both have average winter minimums in the 20- to 30-degree F range, but Florida gets considerable rainfall, mostly in summer, while much of California is near-desert with most rain falling in winter. Plants notice the difference, to say the least.

You can often find zone maps on seed packets. Also, you can find zone maps for North America and Europe in *Gardening For Dummies* (Wiley Publishing).

Bottom line

USDA zone recommendations are handy, but you may need more to go on when choosing plants for your area. Check heat tolerance and other factors with a local nursery. Most nurseries carry the plants that perform well locally, but some gamble (such as selling annuals when frost can still kill them) because customers demand them.

Bottom bottom line

 Here's the biggest caveat of all when growing plants in containers: Plants in containers are more exposed to the elements than plants grown in the ground. To be cautious, expect that plants in containers may not be as hardy as in the ground. To be on the safe side, figure that if you live in zone 5, subtract one or two zones and choose plants that are hardy to zones 3 or 4. Of course, this advice changes if you move container plants into protection during cold weather.

Climates and Container Plantings

When you garden in containers, certain climatic factors are more important than when you grow plants in the ground; the reverse is also true — some climate considerations are less important for container plantings. For instance, the absolute minimum temperature in your area doesn't matter that much if you move a container-grown geranium indoors for the winter. On the other hand, the typical last frost date is even more critical because that's when you can safely move the geranium back out into the garden.

Here's how climate affects basic container plant categories:

Seasonal performers

Our focus on annuals includes tender perennials that are treated as annuals. You generally expect one season from them. For example, plant petunias when warm weather comes, and throw them away when they get tired or hit by cold weather. With annuals like petunias, pay particular attention to the last frost date of your climate. To a petunia, it doesn't really matter that Frostpak City, North Dakota drops to -50°F in winter, just that the last frost is around June 10, when you can start planting. Growing in containers allows you to take some liberties. You can plant petunias before the last-frost date if you can move them under cover on cold nights.

In mild climate locations like southern California, there's a whole other planting season for annuals in fall — more on that in Chapter 6.

Permanent plants: A few words about winter

We're talking mainly trees, shrubs, and vines — many climatic factors affect their projected success in your area.

Year-round container plants are a way of life in mild climates — as common as cell phones in California. But container gardening in cold-winter climates has limitations. The reason, in a word, is *winter*. Even plants that most of us think of as hardy — pine trees, for example — can't survive really cold winters in containers exposed to the elements, although they thrive in the same climate in the ground. Their roots freeze because the pots lack the insulation provided by the ground or they dehydrate as deep frost draws moisture from the soil.

For example, can you grow shrubs and trees all year in container plants in climates as cold as Minnesota in zones 3 and 4? "Forget it," says Deb Brown of the Minnesota Extension Service. She recommends sticking to containers of annuals and perennials during warm seasons only.

Mike Hibbard of Bachman's Garden Centers, also in Minnesota, describes some extreme measures employed by energetic gardeners who want to carry treasured container plants through the winter. He cites the "tip and bury" method that can be used on deciduous plants that are normally hardy only to zone 7 (such as Japanese maple): Tie branches of the plant together after it loses its leaves, lay it on its side in a trench that is 14 inches deep and wide enough to hold the plant, cover the plant with burlap, and then cover the plant, container, and all with soil. When the soil starts to thaw in April or later, dig out the plant, stand it up, start watering, and see if it responds. Yes, this is extreme. We leave it to you to figure out if it's worth a try.

Of course, if you have a greenhouse (or conservatory), you can keep tender plants safe for the winter. Other ways exist to winterize individual plants, none simple, none foolproof:

✔ Bury containers in the ground (watch that they don't become waterlogged).

✔ Wrap the plant with an insulating blanket of straw and chicken wire (pictured in Figure 2-1).

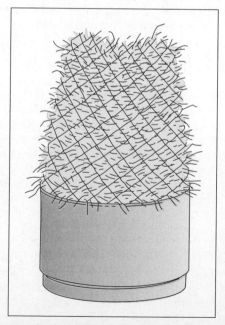

Figure 2-1: A plant insulated with straw and chicken wire.

Again, you need to decide if these methods or other local strategies are worth the effort. Simpler techniques work well in areas where container plants are marginally hardy. In climates like these, try to move frost-threatened container plants under an overhang on a cold night.

As you know by now, figuring out which plants can survive winter in your area is a bit tricky. Check with a knowledgeable local nursery or cooperative extension service before investing much in permanent container plants.

If you live in a cold climate, also remember that winter temperatures can affect your containers as well as your plants. If left outside, terra-cotta pots with soil in them can crack when moist soil expands as it freezes; move pots into protected areas for the winter.

Your Garden's Microclimate

Your own outdoor spaces have particular conditions that you need to consider when planning to grow container plants.

Sun or shade?

Plants have natural attributes that cause them to perform better in different amounts of sunlight. Think about a plant's heredity for a few seconds. What is the best garden location for a vine that's native to the jungle? The logical response: where it's likely to receive protection from the sun like it gets in nature from a high tree canopy. Give the plant too much sun and it burns like an Irish redhead on the beach in Cancun. Or think about a plant with a sunny heredity. Zinnias, originally from Mexico, thrive in full sun. In too much shade, they grow spindly and develop mildew on their leaves.

Most annuals and vegetables do best in full sun, usually meaning about seven hours of sunlight in the middle of a summer day. If a spot in the garden gets its seven hours during the morning or late afternoon when the sun is not as intense, you may have a shortage of required sunlight. For those situations, think about growing shade lovers.

Permanent plants differ widely in their needs for sun or shade, ranging from cactus with a fondness for full sun to ferns that can get along fine in total shade. Try to notice the pattern of sun and shade in your garden. Expect changes with time and the seasons, as the sun moves higher and lower in the sky, as trees grow taller and develop and lose leaves, as neighbors build or tear down buildings.

Here are some points to keep in mind:

- ✔ A northern exposure probably is blocked from the sun all day. This is *full shade*.

- ✔ The east side of your house, unless it's blocked by trees or buildings, receives sun in the morning and shade for the rest of the day. This is a typical *part shade*.

- ✔ Southern exposure gets the most sun. This is *full sun*.

- ✔ A western exposure may get shade in the morning and full sun in the afternoon — usually considered *sunny* because of the intensity of the light (shade plants can cook in this location).

Pay attention to the sun/shade requirements for each plant as recommended by your nursery. Watch for responses to existing conditions. Brown, burned spots on leaves, as shown in Figure 2-2, mean too much sun. A giveaway for too much shade is spindly foliage growth and weak blooming. If you notice those signs, experiment with different plants next time.

Figure 2-2: A leaf with burned spots from too much sunlight.

Near the coast, where it's cool and often overcast, plants generally need more sun than in inland regions. Sun-loving plants like zinnias may not get enough light even in full sun, and the result may be mildew. In cool coastal climates, shade-loving plants like begonias can flourish right out in full sun.

Wind and slope

What about wind? Wind can dry out the soil quickly and rob plants of moisture. Stiff breezes can topple tall plants and break brittle ones. Not much you can do about wind, except be sure to water carefully. Plant shrubs or trees to provide a windbreak if possible. Or find more protected spots.

Hilly terrain can affect weather conditions. A sunny south-facing slope can provide a milder situation — cold air drains away. You may find a hillside garden to be several degrees warmer and several weeks ahead of the neighbor's garden at the bottom of the hill. Low spots collect cold air and can be decidedly chillier than nearby sloping spots.

Reflected heat

Paving, house walls, and other reflective surfaces can warm up a garden. Warming effects can be a positive, but we generally become aware of reflected heat when plants burn up from conditions that are too bright — often from paving around a swimming pool. Even cactus can burn.

Flexibility for Flourishing

Experiment by moving plants around to see what they like. Move flowering plants that aren't blooming well into more sun; move foliage plants that look burned into more shade. Be careful, though, about moving conifers like pines or spruce into shade; they show disinclination by losing needles.

Be ready to change with the seasons. Annual flowers, for example, can start out in the bright full sun of early spring when the weather's still kind of coolish. Your plants may benefit from a move to part shade when the weather heats up.

Chapter 3

Containing Your Excitement

*A*mong the joys of gardening is the opportunity to combine aesthetic challenges and satisfactions with practical science-y stuff. Your definition of beauty and function comes into play when you start choosing the containers and matching them to plants. Whether you buy containers, make them yourself, or improvise; your attention to materials, colors, shapes, and cost can be a great statement about your personal taste.

Approach the process with a horticultural-science frame of mind. Your chosen containers need to be good for the plant's health — the right size, material, and shape.

None of this is difficult. And it's kind of fun.

Types of Materials

Containers are available in a huge variety of materials — especially if you start making your own or finding unusual planter prospects. As you look, be sure to consider at least two key factors: porosity and drainage.

✔ **Porosity:** Some materials used for containers are more porous than others and allow moisture and air to penetrate more readily. Unglazed terra-cotta, wood, and paper pulp dry out faster, but also allow soil to cool by evaporation and to "breathe" (roots need oxygen). Porosity has the effect of drawing away excess water, preventing water-logged soil. Non-porous materials like glazed terra-cotta, plastic, and metal hold soil moisture better, which can be both good and bad — depending on the importance of drainage or water retention to your particular plants (more about this real soon).

✔ **Drainage:** For healthy root development, soil must drain water properly and have enough space for air. Soil that is too heavy or dense can slow drainage; so can lack of a drain hole or a blocked drain hole. If drainage is slow or nonexistent, water may collect at the bottom (it can even stagnate and smell bad); roots can smother and the plant can die. Look for drain holes when selecting containers.

The following materials are used most often for containers these days. Each has its strengths and weaknesses.

Terra-cotta or unglazed clay

Picture a flower pot, and you probably see a plain clay container — the kind Peter Rabbit tipped over while sneaking into Mr. McGregor's garden. Unglazed clay or terra-cotta (Italian for "baked earth") is usually reddish-orange, but is available in tan, cream, black, and chocolate, too. Figure 3-1 shows pots in various sizes. Higher quality pots, with thick walls fired in high heat, last longer. Pots fired at low heat have a grainier texture and weather more quickly — not a bad effect if you want it to look like it was from ancient Rome.

Unglazed clay pots generally offer good value for the money. Their earthy colors and natural surface make the pots look comfortable in almost any garden situation, from rustic to formal. Unglazed clay's porosity allows plant roots to breathe and excess moisture to evaporate — all desirable for many plants. Porosity also means that the soil dries out quickly.

Remember that unglazed clay pots are on the breakable side. Durability depends on how they're fired, ingredients in the mix, and thickness of the walls. Simply by hefting the pots, you can pretty much tell the more durable, thick-sided ones.

In cold climates, terra-cotta pot sides can split when moist soil freezes and expands inside the pot.

Figure 3-1: Some terra-cotta pots.

Glazed clay

Usually inexpensive, these pots come in many more colors than unglazed pots — bright to dark, some with patterns. Many are made in Asia and fit nicely in Japanese-style gardens. They're great in formal situations or to liven up a grouping of plain clay pots. Glazed pots are less porous than unglazed and hold moisture better. They are breakable.

Wood

Square and rectangular boxes and round tubs are sold in many styles and are usually made of rot-resistant redwood and cedar. They're heavy and durable and stand up well to cold weather. Appearance is usually rustic, at home on decks and other informal situations. Wood containers provide good soil insulation, keeping roots cooler than in terra-cotta. Evaporation is also less than with clay pots. Thicker lumber is better — at least ⅞ inch. Bottoms may rot if they stay too moist; raise containers at least an inch off the ground with stands or saucers as described later in this chapter. Treat container insides with wood preservative.

Half barrels are inexpensive large containers. Recycled oak whiskey and wine barrels once filled the bill; now, rustic-looking wooden vessels are made specifically for garden purposes. Barrels can accommodate small trees or larger vegetables (beans, tomatoes, squash).

Bushel baskets also offer a homespun look. To encourage longer basket life, treat them with wood preservative and line them with plastic.

Figure 3-2 shows some wood containers along with a few others you're likely to encounter.

Figure 3-2: Big wooden containers, a trough, and a glazed pot.

Plastic

Many plastic pots are designed to imitate standard terra-cotta pots. Plastic is less expensive, easier to clean, and lighter than terra-cotta. It's also nonporous and doesn't dry out as quickly as terra-cotta, so be careful not to overwater. Watch for poor quality plastic, which can fade and become brittle.

The plastic look isn't for everyone. You can camouflage plastic pots in a group of more decorative pots. Or sink a plastic pot with a plant into a larger pot for an instant facelift without even transplanting.

Other materials

You're less likely to encounter containers made of the following materials, but each has its own appeal:

- ✔ **Cast concrete** is durable, heavy, and cold-resistant.

- ✔ **Paper pulp** is compressed recycled paper that degrades in several years. You can plant pot and all directly in the ground, and the roots grow through it as the pot decomposes. Inexpensive and lightweight, but not handsome, try slipping into larger, more attractive containers. Use where looks don't matter. Excellent for vegetables.

- ✔ **Metal** is a favorite choice for antique and Asian planters. Look for brass, copper, iron, aluminum, and other metal containers at boutiques and antique shops. Make sure drainage is provided.

Improvised containers

Turning mundane items into plant containers is fun — as long as you don't mind hearing from more "sophisticated" gardeners. Figure 3-3 shows some interesting improvisations.

Raised beds

Planting beds built into gardens — made with lumber, brick, or many other materials — actually are a form of container, most likely filled with planting mix rather than garden soil. We're not going to discuss raised beds specifically, but much advice for watering and feeding container plants applies.

Containers of your own making

You can also make your own containers — most likely of wood. Check with a local building supply store for plans and materials. Another simple material is called *hyper-tufa*.

Figure 3-3: You can turn all kinds of stuff into containers for plants.

Container Sizes and Shapes

What's good for the plant? What looks nice? You need to deal with both questions. A pot that's too small crowds roots, cutting off moisture, oxygen, and nutrients that are vital for healthy growth. If the pot is too big, the superfluous soil may stay too wet and can smother the roots.

Rules for ideal container size differ a bit for permanent plants and seasonal plants.

For permanent plants like Japanese maple or conifers, think longer term and choose a pot that looks in scale with the plant when you buy it and allows room for a year or two of root growth. As a rule, when buying a nursery plant, transplant it to a container that is 2 inches deeper and wider than its nursery container. Don't be shy about taking the plants you're buying to the container section of a store to find the best match. Or if you own the container, take it into the nursery to match it up with plants.

Seasonals like annuals and bulbs can be crowded together more closely than plants in the ground, providing much more impact quickly. Crowded conditions can't persist for long, but you can satisfy the tight-quarters demands for extra water and food over your plants' short seasons.

As a rule, figure that if the recommended spacing for ground planting is 10 to 12 inches, container planting translates to 6 to 8 inches apart. As a general rule of scale, if the annuals normally grow 10 or 12 inches tall, provide a pot at least 8 inches in diameter. If the plants grow 2 or 3 feet tall, go for a diameter of 24 inches or a large container like a half barrel.

Container shapes vary. Some are designed for practicality, and others, we can assume, look the way they do because someone likes their appearance. The tapered shape of terra-cotta pots, for example, allows plants to slip out more readily for repotting. Makes sense, right?

Standard pots

Most standard pots — the familiar terra-cotta with rim or plastic versions of the same — are taller than they are wide, allowing the roots to grow deep. This works for most plants.

Small containers, up to 8 inches in diameter, can hold a few annuals or perennials, and a single young permanent plant (a small conifer, for example).

Standard pots up to 12 inches in diameter can hold half a dozen annuals, small perennials, or medium shrubs or vines.

Use larger pots (at least 18 inches in diameter) for bigger shrubs, small trees, bamboo, and mixed annuals/perennials.

Low containers

Sometimes called azalea or fern pots, these containers are wider than tall, typically terra-cotta and sold in diameters from 4 to 14 inches. Use them for shallow-rooted plants — may we suggest azaleas and ferns?

Bulb pots

Usually made of terra-cotta and sold in 6- to 12-inch diameters, these shallow containers are not much deeper than saucers. You can get away with planting bulbs in such a small amount of soil; they have shallow roots, need little soil, and are grown for only one season. Shallow bowls can be used for smaller annuals, but make sure that you provide enough soil for growth, and water and fertilize carefully.

Other shapes

Many other styles are also available: bowls, tapered Spanish pots, and bonsai pots (which are shallow). With all of these, remember to check for drainage and space for roots.

Hanging baskets

For the sake of lightness, hanging baskets come mainly in wood and wire. The wire baskets, lined with sphagnum moss or synthetic material to hold in soil, offer room on the sides for inserting plants — producing a look of overflowing abundance. Pick a diameter of at least 9 or 10 inches, preferably 15 or 16 inches. The most common shape is round, but half baskets to attach to a wall are also useful.

Accessories, at Your Service

You may want to consider a few other container-related items to help grow container plants successfully.

Saucers

These items help keep water from going where you don't want it — onto a deck or patio, for instance. Unwanted water, of course, can damage surfaces: in addition, water draining from containers can carry stains from the soil mix.

A saucer looks better if it matches the container. Clear plastic saucers are inexpensive and fairly inconspicuous. Saucers come in standard sizes, designed to match pots. Select a saucer that's at least an inch wider in diameter than the bottom of the pot.

Elevation

Lifting containers off the ground has several advantages. A tall stand, either purchased or made, can lift plants up for eye-level viewing (see Figure 3-4). But just raising the container up several inches allows water to flow more freely out of the container and promotes better air circulation underneath. Wood rot is reduced, and insect hiding places are eliminated.

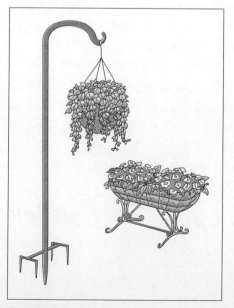

Figure 3-4: Stands raise plants to eye level and promote circulation.

So how do you raise the containers? You can buy decorative "pot feet," sold in many catalogs. You can use three bricks or wood blocks. For just a little lift, you can use hose washers on masonry surfaces.

Feel like improvising? Consider borrowing ideas like a container stand made from an old stool or a water heater base. Take your plants to a higher level with a touch of creativity!

A Pot for Every Plant

For starters, here's a sampling of proven plant-and-container combinations that promise a great look. The containers also deserve note because they're the right size and shape for healthy growth. Read on in this book and you may come up with many other ideas of your own.

- A 10-inch-high golden barrel cactus in a 14-inch-diameter terra-cotta bowl

- English lavender, sweet peas, geranium, sweet alyssum, and catmint in an 18-inch wire basket stuffed with sphagnum moss

- Six water plants (including water lily and Japanese iris) in a water-tight half-barrel filled with water

- Tomato, parsley, and basil in a 16-inch plastic pot

- Dwarf Washington Navel orange tree in a whisky barrel

- Eight dwarf dianthus in an 18-inch ceramic bowl

- A 7-foot black bamboo in a terra-cotta pot that's 12 inches high, 14 inches wide

- Miniature rose and English ivy in an old work boot, size 10 ½ D (we're not kidding!)

Chapter 4

Soil Mixes

● ●

In This Chapter

▶ Getting to know soil

▶ Understanding what container plants really need

▶ Searching out the good soil

▶ Shopping for soil mixes

▶ Making your own foolproof soil mix

● ●

*T*his is the most important chapter in the book! Go ahead, skip this chapter.

Wondering what's going on? The explanation's really pretty simple. If you want to do all your container planting with bags of soil mix bought at the garden center — without having any idea what's in the blend — you can count on reasonably good results. You really don't need to read this chapter.

But if you want to understand what plants need and why — and you may discover that it's fascinating — the place to start is at ground level.

The road to knowledge can be littered with lots of technical stuff. But when you understand how to provide just the right soil for different plants, you open one of gardening's most interesting doors. Make your own soil mix, and you can save money as you customize to create perfect growing conditions for each container plant — and you may enjoy results beyond your wildest imaginings!

So read on, or we'll see you in Chapter 5.

Why Soil Mix Matters

Finding or preparing the right soil mix — one with a perfect crumbly texture that provides plenty of oxygen, plant nutrients, and moisture but that also drains well and is free of diseases, insects, and weed seeds — is the most important thing you can do to ensure the success of your container plants. Because no matter what you plant, an exotic shrub or a simple pot of geraniums, the key to making it work is making sure that your plants are happy beneath the surface.

Why is soil so critical? Because of roots. While we sit back and applaud the flowers and foliage that grow above the rim of the pot, it's the roots underground that are really supporting the show and that deserve our accolades. Roots make up more than half of every plant, and they're working constantly to find the right amount of air, moisture, and nutrients to fuel the flowers and foliage above.

Plants in containers are especially dependent on the soil or growing mix in which they develop simply because there's so much less to choose from in the confines of the pots. So to keep your plants happy and healthy, you need to first take care of the roots. And that means growing them in the right stuff.

Finding the ideal soil mix for container gardening isn't difficult — if you depend on the experts. Fortunately, a whole lot of people study just what plants in containers need. You can go into just about any nursery or garden center and find an aisle with packages marked "growing mix." But to make sense of all the different soil mix products on the market today, or to try your hand at mixing up a batch of your own custom concoction, you must understand what your plants need in order to grow. In this chapter you can dig a little deeper into the underground life of plants and find out just what this pursuit of the perfect potting mixture is all about.

A Quick Primer on Soil

Whether you're discussing the stuff that we walk on and garden in or the bagged commercial products for container growing, soil provides plants with a means of support — a way to hold the plant up — and is a storehouse for the balance of nutrients, oxygen and moisture needed by the plant's roots. But not all soils are created equal, and it's not even recommended that you use outdoor garden soil for container gardening, as we discuss in more detail later. That's right, your good old garden-variety dirt can actually be *bad* for your container plants. However, before you discover the particulars of a good planting mix for container growing, look at what makes up a typical garden soil, just to get some of the lingo down. After you understand the terms, you can move on to the potting mixtures. So sit still for a short course in soil science.

Soil — up close and personal

Healthy garden soils contain a mixture of water, air, and solids (mineral particles and organic matter, or *humus*). The relative percentages of the mineral particles — sand, silt, or clay — determine the soil's *texture*. Here's a closer look at all three components, shown in Figure 4-1:

- ✔ **Sand:** This gritty stuff is larger in size than the other two soil particles. A soil with 70 percent sand particles is classified as *sandy*. Sandy soils drain well and dry out quickly, but don't hold nutrients. One way to recognize a sandy soil: Take a pinch of it and it won't hold together.

- ✔ **Clay:** These particles are so fine, they can be seen only with an electron microscope. Clay soils — classified as containing at least 35 percent clay particles — are sticky to the touch and drain slowly. Clay feels slippery to the touch when you squeeze it together in a ball, and it holds its shape. Clay soils are very high in nutrients, but these often are in forms that are unsuitable for plants.

- ✔ **Silt:** Silt is similar to clay, but the individual particles are much larger, moderating its characteristics. If moist, silt holds its shape fairly well when squeezed together and feels smooth but not sticky. Dry silt feels like flour. Silt holds water and nutrients longer than sand, but not as tightly as clay.

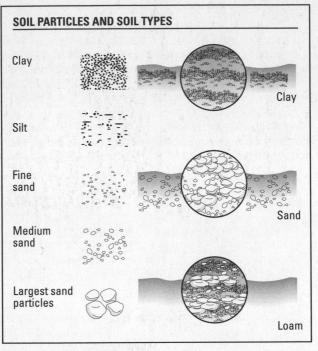

SOIL PARTICLES AND SOIL TYPES

Clay

Clay

Silt

Fine
sand

Sand

Medium
sand

Largest sand
particles

Loam

Figure 4-1: The particles in soil.

Most outdoor garden soils are composed of a combination of all three particles, in varying proportions. *Loam,* which is considered an ideal soil for typical backyard gardening, contains a mixture of sand, silt, and clay as well as plenty of humus (organic material). Loam retains water without becoming waterlogged and contains a balance of the nutrients necessary for plant growth. Formulas for soil mixes presented later in this chapter allow you to create an ideal texture and balance of nutrients for growing plants.

The structured life of soil

The way in which a soil's mineral particles group together determines the *soil structure.* The size and arrangement of these groupings influence the drainage capacity of the soil and its nutrient availability. A very sandy soil, for example, can't form good aggregates (the basic structural units of soil) because its particles are too coarse, and a heavy clay can't form good aggregates because its particles are too fine, causing the soil to be too compact and thereby excluding water and air. Without good drainage, a soil becomes wet and low in oxygen, causing your plant's roots to rot. Drainage is not only important to backyard gardening but is also a *critical* in container growing — more on this in a moment.

When a soil has good structure, it has plenty of spaces for air and water, and lots of room for plant roots to grow in the spaces between the soil aggregates — remember, it's those roots that we're trying to please. In a soil with good structure, the tiny root hairs are able to absorb the air and the nutrient-rich water that help produce the stems, leaves, fruit, and flowers that we cherish so.

Unfortunately, few gardens have true loam soils with an ideal structure. You probably have to make do with a mixture that's too high in clay or sand, and correct it by adding organic matter such as *compost* (garden and kitchen waste that's decomposed to the texture of a crumbly dirt) and nutrients (in the form of compost or fertilizers). Adding organic matter helps form humus, which enables small silt or clay particles to stick together to form larger aggregates; in sandy soils, the humus acts like a sponge to catch and hold moisture and nutrients. Doctoring up the dirt is called *amending the soil* and it makes bad soil better for those all-important roots.

Sweet or sour soil? A word about pH

No discussion of soil science can be complete without a mention of pH, or the relative sweetness (alkalinity) or sourness (acidity) of the soil.

The pH is measured on a scale of 1 to 10, with 7.0 being neutral. A soil pH below 7.0 is considered acidic, while one above 7.0 is alkaline.

The reason a soil's pH is important for plants is that some nutrients are available for uptake by a plant's roots only when the pH is within a specific range. The ideal pH for most plants is 6.0 to 7.0, though a few plants (such as acid-loving rhododendrons, azaleas, blueberries, and some perennials) prefer a slightly lower pH.

Kits for determining pH are readily available in most garden centers, and they're all you probably need for testing soil or your own potting mixes. For the definitive word on a soil's chemistry and makeup, you can order a professional test. Check with your local Cooperative Extension office for more information or for addresses of reputable soil-testing labs.

When buying commercial soil mixes for container plants, you don't have to worry about pH. Mixes in bags are formulated to the correct pH for most plants. Special mixtures are available for ferns, azaleas, or woodland plants that prefer a more acidic soil.

If your garden soil has a pH that is too high or too low, you can correct it. Unfortunately, such a discussion is a bit complex and is really beyond the scope of this book. We can tell you that adding lime counteracts acidity. If you choose to blend your own soil mix, look for recipes later in this chapter that include lime to bring the pH to the right level.

The Perfect Container Mix

Now that you have some soil science lingo under your belt, you can begin to navigate the sea of container mixes. A whole slew of blends are on the market, under a variety of brand names. Some are formulated for starting seedlings, whereas others are geared for potting up transplants or growing nursery stock. But if you look at the ingredients, you may notice is that there's very little real soil, if any, listed.

What gives? Why not use garden soil to grow your prize plants in containers? After all, many of the plants that we raise in containers outside on our patios and decks also grow successfully in the open ground. Why don't we just take a shovelful of soil and dump it in a pot and call it a done deal?

Dirty truths about garden soil

Although it seems to make sense that a good soil in the garden has all the right stuff to make it a good soil in a pot or planter, it just isn't so. Soils that are terrific in the field are not so great when put in containers. When the soil is lifted, it loses its structure. And as garden soil settles in a shallow container (much different from the natural depth of the soil in a field), it forms a dense mass that roots can't penetrate, making it drain poorly and saturating the roots. As a result, not enough oxygen reaches the root zone, and the roots suffocate. Plus, garden soil harbors unwelcome weed seeds and disease-causing organisms that can devastate container plantings.

What container plants need

Plants in containers have different soil and water requirements than plants in the ground and need a special soil mix that meets those needs.

Fast water infiltration and optimal drainage

In garden soil, water is pulled down to the roots by gravity, capillary action, and the attraction of the small clay particles. The water keeps moving through the soil in a continuous column, acting in the same manner that a hose siphon works, or a blotter of ink. Each drop needs another drop of water behind it to continue the flow. Because the soil in a container is so confined, it needs to have a loose, open structure to encourage this flow of water. Plants in garden soil, for example, can grow fine when the rate of water infiltration is as little as ½ inch per hour, but to survive in a container, the same plant needs a water infiltration rate of 5 to 10 inches per hour. How fast a soil drains is known as its *total porosity,* and the higher the number, the faster the drainage.

You know the common advice to put a layer of pea gravel or pot shards in the bottom of your container to improve drainage? Don't do it! Although it may sound logical, using pea gravel in the bottom of a pot actually results in less air for the plant's roots and more water in the bottom of the pot. Instead, fill the entire container with the same soil mix, covering the drainage holes at the bottom with hardware cloth or screen to hold in the soil as needed. Or put the smaller soil-filled pot in a larger decorative pot with gravel in the bottom.

Plenty of air space

Open air goes hand-in-hand with good drainage, and providing breathing space is actually the most important requirement for a good container mix. Container plantings must have plenty of air in the soil after drainage because they require air for growth and respiration (it's those roots again!). A proper container mix has both small and large pores *(micropores* and *macropores)*. When the mix is watered, the water is held in the micropores but drains quickly through the macropores, enabling air to follow. A soil mixture of sphagnum peat moss and *perlite* (a naturally occurring mineral that's used in commercial soil mixes), for example, has more than 20 percent air space after drainage. A typical garden soil may have little space between the soil particles, allowing less than 5 percent air space after drainage.

Determining exactly how much air you need in your potting mixture after drainage depends on what you're growing. Some plants get by with less, others demand an airy environment. Ferns and azaleas, for example, need at least 20 percent air space. Rhododendrons, begonias, snapdragons, and most foliage plants also require high aeration. Vegetables, such as carrots and lettuce, do best with a lighter soil as well. Camellia, chrysanthemums, and poinsettias do fine in an intermediate soil; carnations, geraniums, ivies, and most conifers can tolerate a heavier mix. And for large shrubs or small trees, you need a mixture that has enough weight to keep the container from falling over and retains enough water to support the larger root systems, yet still drains well and provides adequate air spaces.

Moisture retention

Hey, hold it now, you're probably thinking. You just said that container plants need plenty of air and good drainage. Doesn't that message go against holding onto moisture? The logic can be a little tricky. This last requirement — *water retention* — is a tradeoff, because the soil mix that holds onto the most water and drains slowest has less room for air.

Table 4-1 shows how the materials in container mixes vary according to how fast they drain and the amount of water and air left in the soil after drainage. The numbers for water retention and air space are given in percentage by volume; total porosity measures the speed with which a soil drains.

Table 4-1 Characteristics of Container Soil Components

Material	Total Porosity	Water Retention	Air Space after Drainage
Clay loam	59.6	54.9	4.7
Sphagnum peat moss	84.2	58.8	25.4
Fine sand	44.6	38.7	5.9
Redwood sawdust	77.2	49.3	27.9
Perlite (1/16"–3/16")	77.1	47.3	29.8
Vermiculite (0–3/16")	80.5	53.0	27.5
Fir bark (0–1/8")	69.5	38.0	31.5
Fine sand/fir bark (1:1)	54.6	37.4	15.2
Fine sand/peat moss (1:1)	56.7	47.3	9.4
Perlite/peat moss (1:1)	74.9	51.3	23.6

Lack of contamination

Container mixes need to be free of diseases, insects, weed seeds, and harmful chemicals. Garden soil loses out on all counts for container planting. Along with all the clay, silt, and sand that we find in garden soil, a multitude of disease-causing organisms can infect your prize plants. At the time of germination, seedlings are extremely vulnerable to the organisms that cause damping-off and root-rot diseases. But soil contamination can be a factor for larger plantings as well. If you use diseased soil to grow tomatoes, for example, you can expect to end up with rotted fruit rather than vine-ripened beauties. The alternative — pasteurizing the soil with heat — is not easy and definitely not something that you want to do in the house; the odor produced by the process is not pleasant.

With garden soil, you're also getting insects in various stages of development and weed seeds, which flourish in the environment of container plantings. Although weeds may not be such a big deal, bringing insects indoors or into a container area can wreak havoc on the rest of your plants. Finally, it's possible that herbicides or other plant-harmful chemicals may be lurking in field or garden soil, and when transferred to the delicate ecosystem of a container garden, the caustic substances may kill the very plants you're attempting to grow.

Rather than use backyard garden soil, commercial nursery growers (and most gardeners) now turn to soil-less mixes as a basis for their container potting mixtures.

Bring On the Soil Mixes (For Peat's Sake)

The movement away from real soil in potting mixes began more than 60 years ago, in an attempt to eliminate the soil diseases that were plaguing the nursery industry and find an alternative to topsoil, which was being lost to urbanization and herbicide contamination. The first mixes were made of sand or sandy soil mixed with milled sphagnum peat moss. But these concoctions were heavy and still had to be sterilized because of the natural disease organisms present in the sand.

Then in the mid-1950s plant pathologists at the University of California (Go Bears!) developed U. of C. mixes that were uniformly lightweight and disease-free. On the other coast in the early 1960s, researchers at Cornell University produced peat-lite — a half and half mixture of milled sphagnum peat and vermiculite (a natural mineral) — which became the basis of today's commercial soil-less growing mixes. The dozens of companies that now market soil-less mixes each have their own variation of this basic formula, customized for uses running the gamut from seed-starting to nursery plantings. You can find them under the names Fafard Mixes, Jiffy-Mix, Metro-Mix, Pro-Gro, Pro-Mix, Redi-Earth, and many others.

Called *growing media* in the professional nursery trade, the mixes you find at your local nursery, garden center, or superstore today are based on a combination of organic components like *sphagnum peat moss, composted pine bark* or *fir bark,* or other wood by-products, and a mineral fraction such as *vermiculite* and *perlite* (two naturally occurring mineral elements that pop like popcorn when they're exposed to very high temperatures, making them extremely lightweight and porous). Some heavier mixes include sand that has been washed and screened to remove fine particles. Most mixes also contain a small amount of *ground limestone* (usually dolomite) to correct the acidity of the organic component and to buffer alkaline or acidic water supplies; they may include a *wetting agent* (to help moisten water-resistant peat) and a dose of *fertilize*r (to get your plants off to a good start).

Mixes containing high-quality compost and perlite, plus other ingredients like composted manure, are now making their debut as well. Proponents of compost-peat mixtures claim that the naturally disease-suppressive qualities of high-quality compost actually help inhibit soilborne diseases.

Other ingredients used in some commercial mixes include rice hulls, rock wool (a soil-less amendment made from basaltic rock), and coconut coir pith (a coarse outer-husk fiber used as an alternative to sphagnum peat moss). The following list gives a sampling of what you may find in different mixes:

- ✔ **Charcoal:** Used to absorb toxic agents in the mix.

- ✔ **Compost:** Decomposed vegetative matter. Adds nutrients, microorganisms, and weight. Holds moisture. Can be highly variable in quality.

- ✔ **Composted fir or pine bark, redwood sawdust, or shavings:** Lightens the mix by providing better porosity. The ingredients used in commercial mixes are stabilized so that they won't deplete nitrogen.

- ✔ **Dolomitic limestone:** Added to peat-based mixes to correct the acidity of the peat. Supplies some calcium and magnesium to plants.

- ✔ **Fertilizers:** Chemical fertilizers give plants an initial boost, and are included in many soil-less mixes under the term *starter charge*. Seaweed fertilizers are sometimes used for a quick fix in organic mixes, while slower-acting amendments like bone meal or blood meal provide longer-lasting nutrients.

- ✔ **Manure:** May be found in organic potting mixes, usually available in bags. Well-aged, composted, commercial type originates with cows.

- ✔ **Perlite:** A granite-like volcanic rock that expands to 20 times its original volume when heat treated at 1500° to 2000°F. Does not absorb water like vermiculite. Aerates and lightens, improves drainage.

✔ **Sand:** Washed, screened sand (often called builders' sand). Adds weight to the mix and aids water flow.

✔ **Sphagnum peat moss:** High-quality peat that acts like a sponge when moistened, retaining water while also aerating the mix and improving drainage. Basic component of soil-less mixes.

✔ **Topsoil:** May be found in soil-based potting mixes. Usually a select loam soil with 3 to 5 percent humus. Adds weight, provides nutrients, contains microorganisms that may cause disease. Bagged topsoil is best; avoid garden loam.

✔ **Vermiculite:** Processed mineral flakes that expand to 20 times original volume under heat treatment. Retains water and aerates the mix. Breaks down quicker than perlite.

✔ **Wetting agent:** Used to help wet peat moss, which is naturally water-resistant when dry.

Shopping for a soil mix

Picking the most appropriate mix for your planting needs depends on knowing what you want to grow. For starting plants from seed or growing very small (under 4 inches) potted plants, for example, you're best off buying a straight soil-less mix based on peat, vermiculite, and perlite, labeled *seed-starting mix* or *germinating mix*. These mixes are screened to be very fine, ideal for starting small seeds. But they're not good for growing plants in larger containers because they hold too much water and eventually compact, providing too little air for good long-term root growth.

For container gardening in hanging baskets or medium-size containers, you need a coarser mix that has better porosity, labeled *general purpose mix*. The formulations often include composted pine bark for better drainage.

Larger containers that can hold large shrubs or small trees require an even heavier mix (to anchor the pot), but one with adequate drainage and air space for root growth. Such mixtures, sometimes labeled *nursery mix*, often have sand and composted bark mulch added to the peat mix.

Look for soil mixes formulated for plants needing specific conditions: African violets, bulbs, cactus, orchids, and others.

Fortunately, most reliable suppliers describe the contents of their various mixes clearly, with the most common ingredient listed first (often with the percentage), followed by lesser ones in descending order, so that you know what you're getting. If you're still unsure about what to buy, visit your local nursery or garden center and ask which product they suggest.

Where to buy soil mixes

Soil mixes for container growing are sold in plastic bags, either loose (in a size range from 1 quart up to a 40-pound bag) or in compressed bales (weighing about 70 pounds). Compressed bales yield almost twice the volume on the label when you dig out the mix and fluff it up. If you have a large number of plants to pot, it can be more economical to buy the bales than to purchase individual smaller bags of mix.

You can find soil mixes at most places that sell potted plants. Superstores with gardening sections offer a wide choice of brand names, often at bargain prices. Local nurseries and garden centers have a full line of mixes, likely at more expensive prices, but you can get some advice on what to buy. At a retail nursery that propagates and pots up some of its own plants, expect the narrowest selection but potentially the best choice: the mixes the professional growers use themselves. You may be able to buy a soil-mix bag or a bale at a cost above the wholesale price, but less than retail if the grower is willing to sell you some. At the very least, you can ask those experts what they recommend and then match your mix to that recipe (see "Doctoring up the mix," later in this chapter).

Whatever you buy, keep the bag tightly closed so that it doesn't dry out or become infected with disease organisms and protected from rain to prevent saturation and rot. The plastic covering on commercial-size bags and bales is usually treated with ultraviolet light inhibitors, giving the material about a one-year shelf life when stored out in the open. You can store the mix in an enclosed shed or in a dry, well-aired basement, though, to keep it for more than one season.

Mixing Your Own

With a little knowledge of what to look for, you can't really go wrong with buying a commercial mix. And if you plan to grow only a few containers out on the patio or pot plants for indoors, you can purchase a container mix, plant your pots, and then sit back to enjoy the gardens that result. With commercial mixes, you're most likely to get a consistent product that's free of disease — a significant advantage with container plantings. And in some cases, relying on a tried-and-true formula is actually the most economical thing to do.

If you can't find a growing mix that suits your needs, though, and you really want to get down and dirty, mix your own blend. Be aware that you may need to experiment (using the general recipes that follow) to achieve just the right mix. Or you may be able to whip up exactly what you want by slightly modifying a commercial mix.

Doctoring up the mix

Professional nurseries, who generally have plenty of the raw materials on site, often buy wholesale mixtures of a general peat-based growing mix and then customize it to meet their needs. Some growers find the commercial soil-less mixes too dense when used as is and want to lighten the mix with amendments like perlite. Other experts determine that the mixes are too dry for their intended container plants or too light to support larger plantings like trees or shrubs, so they add composted bark mulch, compost or leaf mold (partially decayed leaves), sand, or even high-quality bagged topsoil to the brew. Fertilizers, generally in slow-release forms that are temperature- and water-sensitive, such as Osmocote, are often added to provide nutrients throughout the growing season.

If you add topsoil or other soil-based ingredients to your potting mixture, you run the risk of introducing disease-causing organisms to your container. For best results, use only bagged, commercial topsoil, not the backyard garden fare.

If you're growing large shrubs or even trees in containers, a sterile potting mixture is not as critical as it is for seedlings or small pots. But you're still taking a chance. Also, when you add any amendments to a commercial soil mix, you upset the balance of ingredients that are carefully formulated by the soil mix experts who produce the blend. Perhaps the best course to take if you want to amend a mix is to visit your local nursery or garden center and find out what the folks there recommend for the specific plants you're intending to grow.

Foolproof mixes from scratch

If you've read this far, you probably fit the description of a do-it-yourself gardener — someone who wants to get to the nitty-gritty of all this soil science stuff. Or maybe you're hoping to save some money by mixing your own brew in bulk. The following recipes can start you on your way to developing your own custom concoction. All sorts of combinations are possible; you need to decide if you want a purely soil-less (peat-based) mix or an organic type that contains real soil.

Aim for a mix with an ideal texture, crumbling easily in your hand and providing good drainage and air spaces while retaining adequate moisture. The right stuff also has the correct balance of nutrients and matches the appropriate level of lime or acidity for your chosen plants — slightly acid for most plants, moderately acid for azaleas and other acid-loving plants. The mix needs to be uniform from batch to batch, and free of diseases, insects, weed seed, and harmful chemicals.

A simple combination of peat moss and vermiculite (or perlite or sand), such as the Cornell mix described next, can be used for virtually all plants. Choose the ingredients that best suit your planting program. For outdoor containers receiving frequent rains, use perlite rather than vermiculite. For shrubs or tree containers, add ⅓ part sand and ⅔ ground bark or peat moss for a heavier mix.

Whichever mix you use, follow the same basic method for mixing (described next) and store any leftover mix in plastic bags or a tightly sealed plastic garbage can.

Basic peat mix (Cornell soil-less mix)

This recipe creates one cubic yard of mix. First combine:

> ½ cubic yard of sphagnum peat moss
>
> ½ cubic yard of vermiculite

Dump the ingredients in a pile on a smooth, clean surface like a concrete patio or driveway, or on a plastic tarp where you won't contaminate it (for smaller proportions, use a wheelbarrow or garden cart). Break up the peat moss as needed so it isn't clumped. Mix, adding warm water as necessary to lightly moisten the material, and continue mixing until thoroughly combined.

Now add fertilizers:

> 5 pounds of dolomitic limestone
>
> 1 pound of superphosphate
>
> 2 pounds of 5-10-5 fertilizer

Mix by shoveling all the ingredients into a cone-shaped pile (see Figure 4-2). Repeat the cone building at least three times.

If you don't plan to use the mix immediately, store it, tightly closed, in plastic garbage bags or a clean plastic garbage can.

Variations on the peat theme

For a very lightweight mix for seedlings and small pots, use equal parts peat moss, vermiculite, and perlite (roughly 9 cubic feet of each).

For a heavier mix for seedlings and pots, use 1 part peat moss (about 14 cubic feet), ½ part sand, and ½ part perlite (7 cubic feet each).

For shrubs and trees, use 1 part peat moss, 1 part composted bark, and 1 part sand (9 cubic feet each), or a mixture of 2 parts composted bark and 1 part sand.

WARNING!

Hold those packing peanuts!

Tempted to use those polystyrene packing peanuts in your custom mix? Better not. They're too large, coarse, and lightweight to use in a soil mix. To get them to the right size, you'd have to shred them into ¼-inch pieces or smaller, and the particles are so light that they would migrate to the soil surface and blow away. Stick to perlite instead.

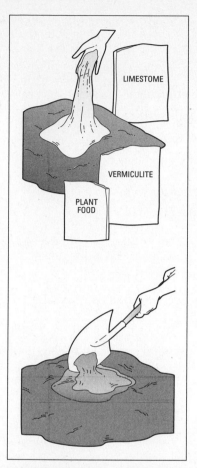

Figure 4-2: Combine the ingredients by shoveling them in a cone-shaped pile.

Two specialized blends

If you prefer to work with organic materials, consider either of these two all-purpose mixes.

A mix from Natural Organic Farmers Association
(Makes 1 bushel of mix.)

> 16 quarts of sphagnum peat moss
>
> 16 quarts of vermiculite
>
> 7 ounces of bonemeal
>
> 3½ ounces of dried blood meal
>
> 3½ ounces of ground limestone

An organic mix based on soil

> 2 parts vermiculite
>
> 2 parts perlite
>
> 3 parts bagged, commercial grade topsoil
>
> 3 parts sphagnum peat moss
>
> 2 parts bagged, composted cow manure
>
> ½ part bonemeal

Chapter 5

When Plant Meets Container

*Y*ou have your container (look back to Chapter 3) and your soil mix (Chapter 4). What's next? Go ahead and stick the plant in the pot? Well . . . there's actually a little more to container gardening if you want to give your plants the best possible start in life — sort of the equivalent to sending them to preschool and kindergarten before elementary school on their way to medical school.

Exactly how and when you plant depends on the plants you choose. In coming chapters, we recommend many plants to grow in containers. Here we cover the basic techniques that work for most annuals, perennials, shrubs, and trees.

What You Need to Know First

Before you stick a plant in a container, try to digest some basic planting advice. If you're already familiar with the fundamentals, feel free to skip ahead a few pages.

Planting seasons

With containers, you follow the same seasonal rhythms that direct planting in the ground. Table 5-1 offers general guidelines for planting in two basic broad climate types.

Table 5-1	When to Plant Various Plants	
Plant Type	*Cold-Winter Climates*	*Mild-Winter Climates*
Perennials	Spring and late summer	Spring, fall, and late winter
Annual flowers	Spring and summer	Year-round
Hardy bulbs	Fall	Fall
Tender bulbs	Spring	Spring
Shrubs and trees	Spring and fall	Year-round
Bare-root (shrubs, trees, fruit trees)	Spring	Winter
Vegetables (cool-season)	Fall, winter, spring, summer	Early spring
Vegetables (warm-season)	Late spring	Summer

How plants are sold

Most people buy plants in convenient nursery packs and pots, transplanting their purchases into various sizes and shapes of containers. But several other excellent ways to purchase plants exist:

✔ **Seeds:** Mail-order catalogs and nursery racks offer seeds of countless varieties of annuals and perennials, and even an array of larger permanent plants. Growing plants from seeds takes time, and because you're unlikely to want huge numbers of the same plants for container gardening, you generally can't take advantage of the money-saving economy of scale provided by seeds. But if you want to cut costs by growing 200 white impatiens for a wedding, follow our seed-starting advice later in this chapter. In that same section, you also find a few plants that are easy to grow from seeds started directly in a container.

✔ **Bulbs:** They're great for containers. Order from catalogs or check your local nursery in fall and spring.

✔ **Bedding plants:** We're talking annual and perennial flowers for summer bloom — and other seasons, too — as well as many vegetables. Seedlings are usually grown by large wholesalers and sold at your local garden center in flats (wooden boxes, almost obsolete now), small cell-packs or six-packs, and small pots (up to 3 or 4 inches or so) — a top choice for most people who plant containers with summer flowers or vegetables.

✔ **Container-grown plants:** Shrubs and trees, along with some larger annuals and perennials, are offered in familiar 1-gallon, 5-gallon, and 15-gallon cans — more often plastic than metal these days. Paper pulp pots, made of compressed recycled paper, are also used for many shrubs and trees but primarily contain larger annuals and perennials.

✔ **Bare-root:** Deciduous trees and shrubs, especially fruit-bearing types and roses, are typically sold when they're dormant and leafless. (Many perennials also are sold bare-root, particularly by mail-order companies.) The plants are dug from growing fields, and their roots are washed of soil — don't worry, survival rate is high as long as the roots don't dry out. Bare-root is one of the more economical ways to buy good-sized plants, and it's a sure way to start plants off right; you can ensure that roots are properly spread out in the right growing medium. After you buy bare-root plants, keep the roots moist until planting by covering with damp peat moss or other organic matter. As you're planting, immerse the roots in a bucket of water to keep them moist.

✔ **Balled and burlapped:** Here's another traditional method that we see less of today. Evergreen shrubs and trees, along with deciduous types that can't be successfully handled bare-root, are dug from growing fields with a ball of soil around the roots, then wrapped with burlap. You can find balled-burlapped plants during the dormant season, often in very large sizes.

How to choose healthy plants

The longer you garden, the better you become at recognizing healthy plants that are ready to take off for a long and productive life in a container. Here are some obvious signs:

- ✔ Younger is better than older, smaller better than bigger. The longer plants stay in nursery containers, the more likely they are to develop a root-bound condition.

- ✔ Deep green is better than yellow or a dull color — realizing, of course, that we're not talking about plants that naturally have yellow foliage or dull leaves.

- ✔ Bushy is better than sparse.

- ✔ Green lively branches are better than woodier growth.

The following pointers can help you select healthy specimens from the two big categories of plants used for containers:

Annuals

Look for bedding plants that are a good green color, appear to have been watered regularly, and are relatively short and stocky.

Plants in small containers cost less than those in larger ones, and you may get more — or less — than you bargained for. Larger plants with more extensive root systems have a head start over smaller plants, but sometimes there's a disadvantage to buying large, fully developed bedding plants. In any container, a plant's roots tend to grow into a thick spiral. If the root situation is extremely crowded, the roots may refuse to spread outward after transplanting. At the nursery, don't be shy about tipping the plant out of its pot or pack and inspecting its roots. Avoid ones with thick tangles of roots searching for a place to grow — such as out the bottom of the container's drainage hole.

What about annuals in bloom? To make seedlings as appealing as possible for sale at the nursery, plant breeders tinker with genes to develop flowers that pop a blossom or two at an early age, and then downshift for a few more weeks of vegetative growth before they start blooming again. In other words, precocious blooming may slow down growth and flower production in the long run. If you buy plants already in flower, pinch off the blossoms when you set out the plants. This preemptive pinching encourages the plants to get on with the business of growing buds and branches.

Seedlings purchased straight from a greenhouse benefit from a short period of hardening off — that simply means acclimating the seedling to its new surroundings, the difference between the comforts of a greenhouse and the cold or heat of an exposed garden bed. As soon as you get seedlings home, place them in a bright, protected place in partial shade, and water them well. After a few days, move them to full sun, and add a little fertilizer to the water. By this time, they're nicely accustomed to direct sun and wind and are tough enough to transplant. If your new seedlings have already spent some time outdoors at the nursery, they can skip the hardening off and go straight into the garden.

Shrubs and trees

Again, avoid the temptation to buy the largest size. Instead look for thick branching and sturdy, well-rounded shape (not one-side growth). Inspect for vigorous new growth at the branch tips and healthy bark (no splits).

The biggest thing to avoid is a root-bound plant — where the roots fill up the container, poke through the drain holes, and don't allow sufficient water to soak in. If a seriously rootbound plant is all you can find, better choose another variety.

When shopping for bare-root plants, check for plump, firm, moist roots. Avoid shriveled, dry, and brittle roots. With balled-and-burlapped plants, check for splits in the ball of soil, which can cause roots to dry out. Make sure the soil ball hasn't dried out; remoistening it thoroughly can be difficult.

Your Well-Stocked Planting Tool Kit

Here are a few reminders and a quick checklist to make sure you have all you need before you start planting:

> ✔ **Container:** Is it the right size (see Chapter 3)? You have to prepare it as described in Step 1 in the following "Basic Planting Steps" section.

✔ **Potting soil:** Make your own or buy it. Include complete fertilizer if you haven't already added it. See Chapter 4.

✔ **Drain hole cover:** Screen or pot shards — see Step 2, which follows this section.

✔ **Shears and knife:** You may need to cut up root-bound roots or trim top growth a bit.

✔ **Scoop:** Use this to move soil mix. A trowel or shovel (for big jobs) also works.

✔ **Gloves:** Handling soil dries out your hands, and you may want leather or cloth gloves to protect them.

✔ **Water:** Your plant needs it as soon as you plant it. Use a watering can or hose (a bubbler attachment helps soften the flow).

✔ **Miscellaneous:** Stakes, plant ties, trellis, snail bait — anything else you may need right after planting.

Basic Planting Steps

Follow these steps for most shrubs, trees, annuals, and perennials. Check specific chapters for details on other types of plants and containers (cactus, vegetables, and so on).

1. Getting the container ready

Make sure the container is the right size (see Chapter 3). Quick reminders: For permanent plants, choose a container that's 2 inches wider and deeper than the nursery container, as shown in Figure 5-1. Bare-root plants need a container that's several inches wider and deeper than the stretched-out, trimmed-up roots — after they're pruned, if necessary, at the nursery. Annuals and perennials can be crowded together more closely than if they're planted in the ground.

Some containers need a bit of preparation. Traditional advice for new terra-cotta pots is to soak them in water for 10 or 15 minutes before planting to prevent clay from absorbing moisture from the soil mix.

If you're using old pots, you may want to clean them to remove salt deposits and reduce chances of disease. And, as logic dictates, it's easier to apply preservativeto wood containers before you plant than afterwards.

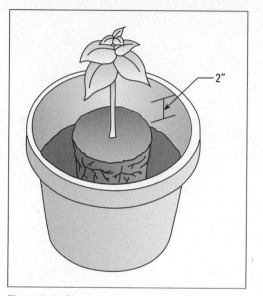

Figure 5-1: Give your plant about 2 inches more in depth and diameter than its nursery container.

2. Addressing the drain hole

Most commercially made pots have drain holes to allow water to flow out of the container. Don't ask why, but these holes usually are too big, allowing too much water to escape.

You need to partially cover the drain holes to keep soil mix from slipping through. Use a piece of fine-mesh metal screen large enough to cover the hole — don't worry about the screen's shape or looks since no one but sowbugs will see it. Or use a time-honored method and cover the drain holes with pot shards (pieces of broken pot), as shown in Figure 5-2. If you don't have any pots you want to smash, use a rock with an uneven shape that doesn't block the hole (a flat stone over the hole stops all drainage).

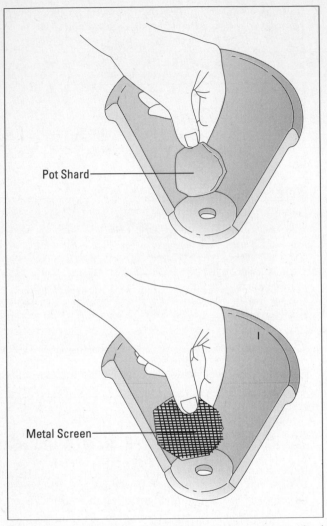

Pot Shard

Metal Screen

Figure 5-2: You can cover a large drain hole with a pot shard (top) or a piece of fine-mesh metal screen (bottom).

If your container lacks a drain hole, you need to make one. Drilling holes in a the base of a wooden box is easy: one ½-inch hole for a box up to 12 inches square; two to four ½-inch holes for larger boxes or a half barrel. For clay pots, use an electric drill with a masonry bit. Support the pot on a block of wood and start drilling with a smaller bit, eventually reaching the final size of ½ inch; adding water to the drill hole may help.

3. Dealing with the plant

Whatever the plant's original residence — nursery can, cell-pack, or paper pulp pot — you need to pay attention to a few key matters before you start the actual planting.

First make sure that the nursery plant's soil is moist enough to hold the roots together when you plant. If the soil is dry, give it a good soaking and let it drain for at least an hour. Soil in the confines of the nursery pack, pot, or can absorbs water better than when it's in a newly planted container — a plant's dry root ball surrounded by fresh soil mix sometimes repels water. (If you're planting bare-root, keep roots moist until the last minute, and just before planting or the night before, immerse the plant in a bucket of water.)

Remove the plant from nursery container, and inspect the root ball. Is it root-bound? Do roots protrude from the drain hole? Or are roots twined around into a dense mass that repels water? For small plants, such as annuals, that may be a bit root-bound, gently loosen the mat of roots with your fingertips. For larger plants, such as 1- or 5-gallon shrubs, use a knife to score vertical scratches in a tight root ball.

> ✔ **Larger containers, such as 1- and 5-gallon cans:** Have the nursery cut open metal cans for you; if you use tin snips, be careful of jagged sharp edges. Tip plastic containers upside down, taking care not to break branches, and let the root ball slip out, catching it with one hand, as shown in Figure 5-3. Tap the rim of the container upside down on a hard surface if the root ball doesn't slip out easily. Wetting the soil makes the process go more smoothly. If the soil mass resists, hack apart the plastic with shears, but don't damage the roots. Paper pulp pots can be treated like plastic; they're easy to cut apart if plants resist slipping out.

> ✔ **Small pots:** Usually, small plastic pots can be held upside down and gently shaken to release root balls. Tap upside down on a hard surface if needed.

> ✔ **Plastic cell-packs:** Turn pack upside down and wiggle the base of each cell. Gently tug, but don't break the stem or loosen the root ball.

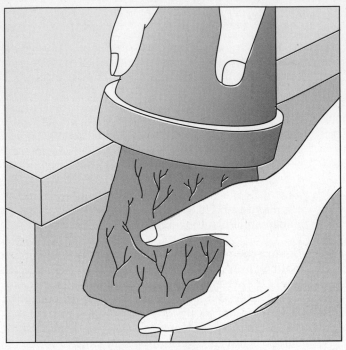

Figure 5-3: Getting a plant out of a plastic container.

4. Planting the plant

Does your store-bought or homemade soil mix include fertilizer? Check the label or your memory. If fertilizer is a part of the mix, don't worry about feeding for at least four to six weeks after planting. If fertilizer is not included, incorporate a complete food now, as suggested in Chapter 4.

Check to see if the soil mix is moist. Bagged may be moist enough already, but if the bag is open or old, the soil may be too dry. Test soil by squeezing it into a ball. Mix is easy to wet while it's still in the bag: Add water and stir or knead until desired level of moisture. Or pile up soil mix and squirt it with the hose, turning it over until it's wet enough.

Add soil mix to your container. Fill to an inch below the rim of the container for small plants, 2 inches or more for large containers — create enough space to hold plenty of water. The amount of soil you add depends on the type of plant:

✓ **For small plants in packs or little pots:** Fill the pot to the level that you want to end up with. With your hands or trowel, scoop out a little hole for each plant, slip in the plant, and firm down around its edges with your fingers. If soil level starts to rise too high, remove some soil. Match the soil level to your plants' previous growing conditions — don't bury too deep or allow root balls to rise above the soil level (see Figure 5-4).

✓ **For plants in gallon cans and larger:** Size up the root ball by placing it in the empty pot. Add enough soil mix to raise the top of the root ball to the desired level in the pot, from 2 to 4 inches below the rim. Set the root ball on top of the soil mix and then fill in around it and tamp it down with your hands, a trowel, or a shovel handle. Tamping down is important to establish firm contact between the root ball and new soil mix. Keep adding soil mix until it levels up with the top of the root ball.

Figure 5-4: This one's planted just right.

✓ **For bare-root plants:** First trim off the root tips as recommended by your nursery or have it done for you (also ask about pruning the top growth back, especially for fruit trees). Mound soil mix at the bottom of the container, spread roots over mound, and adjust level of mound until the plant's former soil line (a faint discolored ring around the trunk) matches up with the desired soil level in the container. Fill around roots until the soil reaches the plant's soil line.

✔ **For balled-and-burlapped plants:** Place the root ball on soil mix at the bottom of container as for plants grown in 1 or 5-gallon nursery cans. Cut away the twine holding burlap in place at the top of the root ball. Fold back and trim away the top several inches of burlap with heavy scissors or a knife — the lower, buried part gradually decomposes. Fill with soil mix around root ball as recommended for container-grown plants.

5. Watering

Pay attention. Watering a just-planted container is trickier than you may imagine. Water tends to follow the path of least resistance and drains quickly through the loose soil mix, bypassing the denser root ball. You walk away thinking that your watering job is done. Days later, you realize that the root ball never really got wet and the plant is desiccated. Protect against this by watering *thoroughly* the first time.

The secret to successful watering is a slow, gentle stream. Use a watering can, hose gently trickling, or hose-end bubbler to soften the flow. Slowly fill the pot to the rim and repeat several times. Probe fingers to find out if the root ball has absorbed water — if you can't detect moisture, soak it again.

6. What else?

A number of other necessities require attention:

✔ Apply mulch to shrubs and trees that have a lot of exposed soil, improving appearances and helping conserve water. Use stone or bark chips or other organic matter. Use mulch size in scale with container and plants — no boulders or big chunks of wood.

✔ Stake and tie trees or tall annuals or perennials.

✔ Add a trellis to the container for vines that need support.

If at First You Want to Seed

Just a few types of plants do well from seeds sown directly in the containers where you want them to grow. Stick with fast-growing, easy-care types like marigolds, zinnias, and lettuce. Follow seed packet directions for sowing in the ground.

Most seedlings grow better if they're started in small containers and then "moved up" — transplanted into gradually larger containers. Seedlings just don't perform well if grown in an excessive amount of soil mix.

If you want to grow large quantities of annuals from seed, you can easily start them indoors and gradually transplant up to your final containers. Seed-starting kits and equipment are available at garden centers and in catalogs. Mainly, you need trays or flats, cell-packs, or other small containers, along with special seed-starting soil mix.

1. Fill containers to the top with sterile soil-less mix (see Chapter 4), level the top by sweeping across it with your hand or a table knife, and use your fingertip or a pencil to make small depressions for seeds. Depth need not be exact, but try to plant about three times as deep as the seeds are wide. Drop one or two seeds into each depression, cover with pinches of seed-starting mixture, and dampen thoroughly with plain water. To keep from flooding out the planted seeds, either use a pump spray bottle to mist the containers repeatedly or place the containers in small pans or trays and fill the pans with 1 inch of water. The containers absorb the water in about an hour.

2. To keep the planted containers from drying out, cover them lightly with plastic wrap or enclose the whole tray in a large plastic bag. Keep the containers in a warm place and start checking for germination after three days. As soon as the first sprouts emerge, remove plastic and move the seedlings to good light.

3. Most of the time, you end up with way *too many* seedlings. If left alone, they become so crowded that they can't grow well, so retain only two or three seedlings in a container 2 inches across. Pull out the extras with your fingers or tweezers or dump out the

container on its side, tap the mass of roots to make them fall apart, and gingerly transplant the tiny seedlings to individual containers filled with sterile soil-less mix. As long as you handle young seedlings by their leaves and *never, ever* touch their tender stems, they transplant very easily. If anyone asks, the process of pulling apart and transplanting very young seedlings is called *pricking out*.

4. When seedlings are about two weeks old, they're ready for a little fertilizer. Use one that can be mixed with water and mix at half the strength recommended on the package. Fertilize seedlings about once a week, or every other time that you water them.

5. After four to six weeks, your seedlings are big enough to move outside. To get ready for the big move, spend a week or so getting them gradually accustomed to outdoor sun and wind. Set them outside for a few hours at first, then for a day, then for several days before you transplant them to outdoor containers. This process, called *hardening off*, makes a huge difference in how well seedlings grow after they're transplanted.

Replanting

Eventually plants outgrow the containers they're in. Repotting them is no big deal. With a few basic tips, you can quickly become an expert at recognizing what needs to be repotted, when moving's in order, where to relocate, and how to give your planter royal treatment for a healthy new life.

With repotting, you have two goals. First, many plants need to go into larger containers to allow room for increasing growth as they head toward maturity. With others, repotting can reduce or slow growth so that plants stay happy and healthy in the same size container.

What, when, and where?

Any plant that has restricted roots obviously needs more space. If you see lots of roots coming through the drain hole or find matted roots near the soil surface, it's time for a move.

Repotting applies to long-term plants as well as annuals that you start from seed or small transplants that need space for more and more roots. How often does the need arise? Good question. A general rule is every few years with permanent plants, as often as every month or so with seasonal bedding plants and annuals.

Timing depends on the kind of plant. Permanent plants are best repotted when growth is slow or when they're dormant, well before or after flowering. With this schedule, plants have a chance to recover from these rather dramatic changes. Repot spring blooming permanent plants in fall, evergreens in spring or fall, and spring-flowering bulbs in fall. For summer-flowering bulbs, repot in winter or spring. With bedding plants and annuals, repot as needed through the growing season before the full flush of flowering hits.

To increase growth, you need to give plants more room for roots by transplanting into larger pots. How much larger? Well, moving up little by little to a new pot that's only a few inches larger in diameter is advisable. If you want to control growth and keep the plant from getting too big, you need to trim the roots and return the plant to a pot of the same size.

How do you repot?

Follow the same steps that you apply to regular planting, but first you have to get the plant out of its current home. This may be easy, or it may take some effort if the root ball is a tangled mess. Turn the container upside down, tap the rim, and slide the plant out. In some cases, you may have to trim off large roots poking through the drain hole. For plants going into larger containers, gently pull apart tangled roots, then set the plant in its new or newly filled existing pot. For some permanent plants, you need to go further than teasing apart roots — a little root-pruning's probably in order.

What is root pruning?

Just what it says — using shears to cut away root growth. Do this on pot-bound plants after they reach a desired size. Root pruning controls growth and forces plants to grow new roots, leading to limited but healthy new growth. To do it properly, remove about a quarter of the soil and untangle as much root mass as you can. Using shears, cut between one-half and one-third of the roots. For tightly balled roots, slice off a half inch all around the outside and make vertical cuts top to bottom in several places. Do this without flinching. Snipping away at a living organism may seem harsh, but in the long run you're helping the plant and new roots to grow. Really, you are — the roots' response can be confirmation! Your repotting will likely go off smoothly, but here are tips to help avoid trouble:

✔ Be aware of the obvious signs that repotting's required: poor flowering, quickly dried out soil, stunted leaves and stems, and even leaf drop and die-back (parts of the plant turn brown and die). Plants give these signals because they're not able to draw enough nutrients and moisture from their current root situation.

✔ With large containers, let the roots dry out first (this tends to shrink them) before removing the plant. Always let gravity help and pull by gripping the main stem or trunk. You may need to use a rubber mallet to tap the sides if the root mass is stubborn. And for some, sliding a knife down the sides and around the pot can help.

✔ When the plant goes back into the same pot, take the time to thoroughly wash the pot using hot water and even a 5 to 10 percent bleach solution to remove bacteria.

✔ If you can't get to a complete repotting job, a temporary solution is to replenish the top few inches of potting soil with fresh potting material and a little added fertilizer.

✔ Protect ceramic and clay pots from chipping or cracking by wrapping an old towel or piece of carpeting around the outside before you tilt and tap the sides.

Chapter 6

Annuals

*W*hat's the first thing that you think of when you picture container plants? Probably a geranium, or maybe a petunia — both annual flowers. What's the first colorful container plant right out of the chute in early spring in cold-winter climates? Probably a pansy, again an annual. Bring to mind some of the spectacular container gardens in public spaces, like the hanging baskets in Victoria, British Columbia, or the year-round colorful containers at Disneyland or Disneyworld, and you may focus on the fact that the flowers are annuals — impatiens, marigolds, lobelias, and other familiar garden friends.

Annuals flowers — popular, fun, easy to grow, and universally loved — are just the right plants to consider when talking about container gardening. They're apt to be the first plants that you grow in containers. Yet annuals are so varied and abundant, you may never get tired of growing them.

In this chapter, we point out the many reasons to grow annuals in containers, describe the special care needed that's a bit different from growing the same plants in the ground, and then look at annuals that are particularly well-suited to container life.

What's an Annual?

First, the requisite botany book definition: An annual is defined as a plant that propagates itself by seed and undergoes its life cycle in one growing season. For example, a marigold seed sprouts in May, grows quickly, blooms all summer, dies when frost hits in fall, and scatters seeds that sprout the next year to repeat the process. Compare an annual with a perennial, which usually blooms in its second year and lives for at least a few years. And technically there also are biennials, which usually bloom in the second year and then scatter seed and die.

The nursery definition is more practical: Annuals are one-season plants, typically sold in six-packs and small pots, planted in spring for bloom in that spring, summer, and fall. (In mild climates, you can plant annuals in fall and winter — more on this later.)

Some plants labeled as annuals actually are perennials, but they typically bloom that first season then die when cold weather hits. The geranium is a classic example — it's sold as an annual in cold-winter climates but can live over from year to year and become shrublike in mild climates. And some biennials, such as foxgloves that can bloom the first season, are also considered to be annuals.

At most nurseries, you may not even see the word annual used. More likely, the plants are tagged as bedding plants because of their traditional role in planting beds. Don't pay too much attention to the bedding label — most of these plants grow just fine in pots, as well as in beds.

Why Grow Annuals in Containers?

You may want to grow annuals in containers for a variety of reasons, among them:

- ✔ Annuals are just plain fun to grow. They have the brightest, most appealing flowers, which attract children, butterflies, and just about anyone who wanders past.

✔ Annuals are movers. They grow fast and bloom when young, even while they're still in the nursery packs, which is not always such a good thing (more on this later).

✔ Annuals give you the longest season of abundant bloom of any plants.

✔ Annuals are relatively inexpensive, especially if you buy small plants. If you make mistakes, you can pull out the plants and may even have enough time to replant.

✔ Annuals are responsive. You start to feel like you can read their minds. Provide them with good care and you see the results — lush leaves, lots of flowers, a long bloom season. Give them too little water and the plants dry up right away. Give them too little food, and leaves start to turn yellow. You can correct all these conditions nearly as quickly as you created them — as long as you haven't gone so far as to kill the plants.

✔ With containers, you can put your favorite annuals where they can be best appreciated: sweet peas (yes, even sprawl-prone sweet peas) where you can smell their fragrance; Johnny-Jump-Ups where you can view their tiny splotched faces.

✔ With containers, you can keep annuals out of sight when they're not doing much — as they grow up before blooming or dwindle away after blooming.

✔ You can rotate blooming containers of flowers by the season. Start with spring bloomers like pansies, follow with summer petunias, and then try fall asters. In mild-winter climates, you can also grow containers of annuals that bloom from fall through spring — Iceland poppies are a great choice.

✔ Nothing dresses up a deck or patio faster for a party than blooming annuals brimming from decorative pots.

Strategies for Growing Annuals in Containers

Nothing's simpler than planting annuals in pots: Go to the nursery, put whatever looks good in the shopping cart, buy a pot and a bag of potting mix, take it all home, and put it together. That's often plenty good enough.

But do try to pick up tips about what annuals to look for, when, where, and how to plant them, and how to combine different varieties. You may be surprised at how much you enjoy the process and the results.

Timing is everything with annuals. In typical cold-winter climates, the season for growing annuals is spring to early fall. In mild-winter climates, annuals can thrive year-round. So when do you shop for annuals and plant them? That depends on your climate and whether the annuals are hardy or tender.

Hardy annuals can stand a varying amount of frost, from a little to a lot; some types, in fact, are quite hardy and are actually perennials that live over the winter in many areas. Hardy annuals considered as cool-season annuals perform best when temperatures are mild, days are short, and soil is cool, typically in early spring and early fall. Their enemies are hot weather and long days, which cause a decline in performance and seed setting — ending the bloom season. Examples of cool-season favorites are calendulas, pansies, and snapdragons. You can usually plant hardy cool-season annuals safely a few weeks before the average date of the last spring frost in your area.

Freezing temperature damages or downright destroys tender annuals. Many of these tender types thrive in hot summer weather and are considered warm-season annuals; examples are celosia, marigolds, vinca rosea, and zinnias. Plant them after the date of your last frost — and when soil and air temperatures are warming up. Count on them to reach their peak in midsummer.

Cool-season and warm-season are, of course, relative terms. Where summers are cool, like along the foggy California coast or other overcast climates, you can grow cool-season annuals all summer. Where winters are warm and nearly frost-free (as in low-elevation Arizona and much of California), fall through spring is an ideal stretch for growing cool-season annuals like Iceland poppies and even some warm-season annuals like petunias.

Annuals can be grown all year in several locales — places that boast climates where winter temperatures rarely drop much below freezing.

In mild-climate regions, you can plant cool-season annuals like pansies and Iceland poppies in late summer or early fall (after summer cools off). Blooms may appear before Christmas and peak in late winter and early spring. After growth and flowering slows down in spring, replace them with warm-season annuals.

In these climates, cool-season annuals can also be planted through the winter and early spring. The plants miss out on fall's warm weather to push them into growth but they surge as soon as temperatures start to warm in late winter and early spring.

 Truly tropical climates like those found in Hawaii and southern Florida are in a separate category and have their own special rules for growing annuals. Better check with local nurseries for exact timing.

Shopping for Annuals

A fair bet is that you decide to plant containers with nursery transplants rather than seeds. Transplants make it easier for you, and they're not expensive when used in the quantities that most people buy for containers. (Actually, some annuals are easy to start from seeds sown right in containers if you're so inclined; good choices for seed sowing are cosmos, marigolds, and zinnias.)

Nurseries typically offer the greatest variety of annuals in six-packs containing a half-dozen seedlings or in 4-inch pots containing single plants. Look for plants that have a good green color and are relatively short and stocky. Start with small plants — their root systems adapt quickest to growing in new conditions. If you want color right away, buy larger, blooming plants in pots, gallon cans, or even larger containers. Just be sure that the roots haven't filled the nursery container to the point of shedding water. At the nursery, don't hesitate to tip the plant out of its pot or pack so that you can inspect the roots. Avoid plants with a thick tangle of roots.

Many small transplants sold these days already come with flowers — thanks to clever plant breeders successfully developing annuals to bloom precociously and tempt you into buying them rather than the more laggardly all-green seedlings.

Blooming as a youngster actually impedes future blooming. Snip off the flowers before or just after you plant.

Planting Annuals in Containers

An annual grown in a container needs the same things that a plant in the ground does — mainly water, air, and nutrients. Please remember that roots in a container are confined and can't forage. Careful watering and feeding are essential. Equally important is starting off with a good soil mix — not dirt dug up from your garden — whether you buy it in a bag or mix it yourself. See Chapter 4 for more information on soil mixes.

Choosing containers

What kind of containers are recommended for annuals? Anything goes — that's especially true with annuals. There are so many kinds of annuals, so many colors, shapes, and sizes, and so many different kinds of looks that your container choices are truly wide open.

Here are a few possibly obvious, certainly worthwhile rules:

- ✔ Put tall annuals (gloriosa daisy, cosmos) in big pots.
- ✔ Grow sprawling or spreading types (impatiens, petunias) in low bowls.
- ✔ Terra-cotta pots look great with annuals in almost all situations.

Glazed pots can add even more brightness. Thinking about putting pink petunias in a bright orange glazed pot? Works for us, but don't expect *Garden Design* magazine to come calling.

Now, on to more concrete advice on the practical matters:

- ✔ To grow healthy annuals, the container needs to be at least 6 inches deep.

✔ As a general rule of scale, if the annuals normally grow 10 or 12 inches tall, provide a pot with a diameter of at least 8 inches. If the plants grow 2 or 3 feet tall, better go for a diameter of 24 inches or a large container like a half barrel.

✔ Seasonal plants like annuals can be crowded together more closely than is suggested for ground planting. Cramped conditions can return a much greater impact quickly. Annuals can't grow in crowded conditions for long, but their season is short, and you can satisfy the demand for extra water and food that the tight quarters create. If the recommended spacing for ground planting is 10 to 12 inches, in a container you may space the plants 6 to 8 inches apart. Again, as a general rule, you can safely plant most annuals 4 to 6 inches apart.

Actually planting something

Are you ready to plant? Have you assembled your containers, soil mix, and seedlings? Time to get started:

1. **Before removing plants from their nursery containers, make sure that their root balls are moist.**

   If soil feels dry, soak plants at this point; a root ball can absorb water in the confines of the nursery pack better than in the wider expanse of your planter. Watch for signs of root-bound seedlings: small white roots woven together so tightly that they repel water. Gently loosen roots at the bottom and sides of the root ball.

2. **Deal with drain hole as described in Chapter 5.**

3. **Fill the container to within 2 or 3 inches of its rim with moistened soil mix (wet enough to form a ball when squeezed, but not dripping).**

   Smooth soil level with your hands.

4. **With a trowel or your hands, scoop out a planting hole for each seedling, as shown in Figure 6-1.**

   Make the hole deep enough so that the top of the seedling's root ball is at the same level as the soil in the container.

5. **Place the seedlings in the holes you made, as shown in Figure 6-2.**

   Use your fingers to tamp down soil around each seedling, again ensuring that the root ball's soil level matches the soil level in the container.

6. **Water gently with a watering can or hose until the soil is thoroughly moist.**

Most annuals benefit from full sun, but even sun-lovers can use partial shade right after planting. Keep the containers in partial shade for at least a few days after planting — until they toughen up a bit.

The Caretaking of Annuals in Containers

More than anything else, remember that annuals like to set a fast pace with no pit stops: Running out of water or food can set them back for weeks or abruptly end their seasons.

Watering is much more critical with annuals grown in the confined spaces of containers. Never let the soil dry out. You may want to install a drip system (discussed in Chapter 10) if you have many containers.

Feeding container-grown annuals is also more critical than nourishing the same plants grown in the ground. Start feeding a few weeks after planting. One proven method is to use liquid fertilizer at half the recommended rate and twice the frequency (every two weeks instead of monthly, for example).

Pinching and deadheading are important chores. This caretaking keeps new flowers coming for as long a season as possible. Start pinching back tip growth to encourage bushy growth as soon as you plant, or even right before. Cosmos, marigolds, and zinnias are among many annuals that respond noticeably to pinching; they also produce many more blooms if you constantly remove dead flowers.

Figure 6-1: Scoop out holes for each seedling.

Figure 6-2: Place the seedlings in the holes.

Foolproof Annuals for Containers

When choosing plants for containers, pay special attention to their eventual sizes and growth habits. In general, compact varieties perform better in containers (sunflowers are perhaps the most extreme example, with the 10-foot Russian Giant out of the question and the 24-inch Teddy Bear perfect for containers). Look for special varieties developed for containers. Names often provide a clue to container performance. Cascade petunias, for example, are designed to spill from pots.

Some annuals look great when planted alone; others are mixers that work well when used in combinations with other annuals, perennials, or bulbs.

Old reliables for sunny spots

Here are some favorite annuals to grow in containers alone or combined with other annuals. Of course, annuals are versatile, so feel free to try other ways to use them.

- **Ageratum:** A full pot of ageratum may not be your cup of tea, but it's a great plant to edge a container of mixed annuals. Puffy little flowers most typically are blue, but white and pink also are available. Plants range up to 2 feet tall. Look for dwarf varieties such as Blue Mink.

- **Calendula:** Here's a great choice for containers early in the year. Sturdy plants and bright orange or yellow blooms stand up well to cool weather. Dwarf varieties are best suited to containers.

- **Cineraria:** This one's a spectacular choice for cool-summer climates. Plants are nice and compact, up to 15 inches tall, with clusters of daisy flowers that look like perfect pre-assembled bouquets.

- **Cosmos:** Lacy and elegant, tall cosmos (up to 4 feet) stand out in borders and can also perform in large containers (half barrels, for example). For smaller containers, look for more compact or dwarf varieties. The daisy flowers come in a range of purple, pinks, and whites.

- **Dahlia:** You want compact bedding dahlias, not the tall pot-toppling varieties (unless you grow them in a huge container). Dwarf dahlias grow about 12 to 15 inches tall, with 2 or 3-inch flowers in bright clear colors: orange, pink, purple, red, white, and yellow.

✔ **Dusty Miller:** This is a role player if there ever was one. Its role is to make other plants look good. Silvery gray foliage circling a container's outside edge beautifully sets off purple petunias, red impatiens, or many other annuals and colors. Plants grow about 15 inches tall.

✔ **Geraniums:** We can't think of any geranium that isn't a candidate for good healthy living in a container. Ivy geraniums are a favorite choice for hanging baskets; Summer Showers is specifically designed for hanging. Scented geraniums are fun in pots placed where their foliage can be pinched off for sniffing.

✔ **Iceland poppy:** A cool-season stalwart, its crinkly flowers in bright oranges, pink, yellows, and other shades stand tall on long slender stems, but the plants are low and unprepossessing — best mixed with spreading plants that can provide some camouflage. Pansies are good container companions.

✔ **Lobelia:** Call on the compact edging types (Crystal Palace) to tuck into mixed plantings. Use the trailing types (Sapphire) to spill from hanging baskets or pots. Flowers in light to deep blue, as well as white and lavender, lend themselves to color-combining with many other annuals.

✔ **Marigold:** The tall types are best left in the ground, but the more compact French marigolds and signet marigolds (12 to 20 inches) are indispensable container classics. Fill a pot with a single variety or combine marigolds with other annuals. Colors include yellow and orange, by all means, plus mixes of orange, yellow, maroon, dark red, and more.

✔ **Nemesia:** Feel good about trying nemesia if you live in a cool-summer climate. Otherwise it's pretty fussy. Flowers are richly and vividly colored in red, yellow, white, and pink. Plants grow 8 to 18 inches tall — great near the rims of containers where they can spill over the sides.

✔ **Ornamental kale:** Grow it for striking multicolored foliage — not flowers — early in the season when color is hard to come by. Show off a single plant in an 8-inch pot, or put several in a larger container.

✓ **Pansy and Viola:** Hardy and carefree, these are often the first annuals you notice in containers each spring. Pansies have big, blotchy flowers. Violas are usually solid colors — yellow, blue, purple, and more. Combine pansies or violas with bulbs or fill pots with single or mixed colors.

✓ **Petunias:** Standouts for containers are big-flowered Grandiflora types, especially Cascade and Supercascade strains (they're great spillers). Or try much more compact, smaller-flowered Millifloras such as Fantasy. If plants get too rangy in containers, cut stems back by about a third.

✓ **Salvia:** Scarlet sage, with its bright red spikes of bloom, is an attention-getter in borders or containers. More useful is *Salvia farinacea* Victoria, 24 inches tall, with deep blue flower spikes; this is an ideal choice to plant at the center of pots and surround with lower-growing annuals.

✓ **Snapdragons (dwarfs):** Tall types are too big for most containers. Look for dwarfs such as Little Darling and Royal Carpet — bushy types that grow about a foot tall, with flowers on short stems (unlike long stems on tall types). Don't plan on cutting flowers for bouquets. Snapdragons bloom best in cool weather.

✓ **Sunflowers:** Really. Bushy dwarf varieties grow only 1 or 2 feet tall and are terrific in containers. Two top choices: Dwarf Sungold and Teddy Bear. Sunflowers are easy to grow from seeds started directly in the containers.

✓ **Sweet alyssum:** Low and spreading, this is a dependable choice for filling in among mixed annuals in a pot or spilling over edges of a pot. Sweet alyssum is easy to grow from seeds or transplants. Familiar white is a great complement in mixed plantings, but rose and purple varieties are also available.

✓ **Sweet pea:** The familiar tall, climbing sweet peas quickly grows out of bounds in a container. Bush types, such as Bijou, make a fairly restrained container plant, growing only 12 to 30 inches tall. Flowers come in the usual pastel shades — with a heavenly fragrance.

✓ **Transvaal daisy (Gerbera):** Look for this elegant, deeply colored daisy sold blooming in pots. Transplant a few into a larger container, put them on the front porch or wherever you can appreciate their beauty, and let nature take its course. This is a beautiful temperamental plant; don't take it personally if the daisy fails on you.

✔ **Vinca rosea:** Take a lesson from shopping centers and other public spaces where you see vinca rosea in the hottest spots. This is one tough, heat-loving annual for containers that must face hot sun. Foliage always looks sharp and glossy. White and pink flowers bloom over a very long season.

✔ **Zinnias:** Mix the colors or use single colors for bright containers in full sun. Compact dwarfs, such as Peter Pan, work best in containers. Avoid tall, lanky types. Zinnias come in hot colors and do well in hot weather.

Annuals for shady locations

Color is harder to come by in shady spots, but a handful of annuals thrive in containers and will bloom well in light to medium shade.

✔ **Bedding begonia:** For a neat, well-groomed look, fill pots with solid-colored begonias. Or use them to edge large pots of mixed annuals. Flowers come in red, pink, and white; glossy leaves may have tints of bronze or red.

✔ **Browallia:** This is a beautiful blue trailing plant. A number of new varieties are available specifically for hanging baskets. Look for Blue Bells Improved.

✔ **Coleus:** Colorful foliage can brighten up dark parts of your garden, and provide a tropical look. Combine with shorter shade-lovers like impatiens.

✔ **Impatiens:** Tall or compact, single or double, just about all impatiens perform brilliantly in containers, including hanging baskets. Flower colors include red, pink, rose, violet, orange, white, and bicolors. Double-flowered varieties are especially nice in containers where you can admire the blooms up close. Plant just one color to a pot for the boldest look. Impatiens combine beautifully with ferns, coleus, begonias, and other annuals in mixed plantings.

Combining Annuals in Containers

Combining different annuals in the same container is an easy way to create rainbows of color. The possibilities are infinite. Following are a dozen suggestions for combinations made up of basic plants that look terrific together and have compatible needs. The plants bloom at the same time, their colors contrast or complement each other beautifully, and they're in scale with one another. Some ideas:

- Blue ageratum and pink petunias

- Blue ageratum and yellow marigolds

- Red impatiens and gray dusty miller

- White cosmos and blue lobelia

- Yellow violas and white sweet alyssum

- Blue salvia (*Salvia farinacea* Victoria) and yellow dwarf marigolds

- Coleus and impatiens

- Pink bedding begonias and blue lobelia

- White impatiens and red begonias

- Yellow marigolds, gray dusty miller, and blue lobelia

- Blue salvia, dwarf marigolds, and nemesia

- Pink geraniums, purple violas, and white sweet alyssum

Chapter 7

Perennial Pleasures

*W*hy bother with perennials when annuals (Chapter 6) bloom for a much longer season and have less demanding lifestyles?

As much as we hate to resort to such a vague and overused word, we have to say that perennials are *interesting*. And that's the main reason you grow them. They're interesting in the range of their flowers – from tiny fragrance-packed lavender to towering blue delphiniums. They're interesting in their sheer numbers and variety — thousands of available kinds, including grasses, shade plants, foliage plants, plus some of our more spectacular blooming plants (chrysanthemums and primroses, to name just two). And perennials are interesting in the challenges they present: how to cut back, how to divide, what to do with them in the winter — you don't just relegate them to the compost pile at the end of the season as you do with annuals.

Defining Perennials

Right up front you need to know that we're talking about a specific type of perennial: herbaceous flowering perennials. These perennials have soft fleshy stems (as opposed to a sturdy woody trunk like an oak tree), bloom with worthwhile flowers, and live for several years under the right conditions. Perennials represent a huge and storied population of plants — the subject of their lives now reaches beyond magazine racks and library shelves to the World Wide Web, where they're covered in an abundance of Web sites, discussion groups, and electronic ordering opportunities.

Some perennials are *deciduous*. That means they lose their leaves at some point in the year, usually in winter, or they die back completely to the ground.

Other perennials are *evergreen*, especially in mild climates. Some stay evergreen in mild climates but die way back — or just plain die — in cold climates, where they're considered annuals. One example is the geranium, which is grown as an annual in most parts of the country. In mild places, such as Southern California, geraniums thrive like permanent shrubs — so much so that they're known by the nickname "rats of the garden." So is the geranium annual or perennial? In this book you can locate the universally popular plant in Chapter 6.

Perennials generally have one main blooming season, usually in spring or summer, that can be as brief as a few weeks or as long as a couple of months. Again, evergreen perennials in mild climates can be the wild cards — blooming every month of the year, as a marguerite daisy does.

Enough botany class! What can *you* do with perennials?

Deciding to Pot Your Perennials

Ask a gardener why he or she loves perennials in containers, and here's what you can expect to hear:

- ✔ **Time, money, and labor:** Many gardeners prefer to fill their pots with perennials simply because the plants can last a long time. There's no need to replant pots every few months as you often must do with annuals.

- ✔ **Size:** Perennial plants tend to grow larger than annuals and bulbs, and so can fill large spaces if you want.

- ✔ **Usefulness:** Do you have a spot under the eaves where nothing ever grows? A long wooden staircase that needs some livening up? A blank wall with no soil at the base for planting? In any of these situations, you can use a pot of annuals for bright, perhaps short-lived flowers, but if you want something with interesting flowers, foliage, or fruit over several seasons or years, try perennials.

✔ **Growing the unusual (or temperamental):** If your garden beds are too sunny for hostas or your soil too cold and wet for lavender, try growing them in containers so that you can customize their environments.

Alas, there *are* a few downsides to growing perennials in pots:

✔ **Down time.** Just as we all look a little ratty from time-to-time, a perennial plant sometimes seems out of season — like when it's not blooming or when its leaves fall off. Don't toss (or compost) the unsightly plant. Simply move its pot to a location hidden from view but where you can still provide care until it returns to presentable shape.

✔ **A bit more care.** Perennials in pots require more monitoring than annuals do. You must provide year-round care including fertilizing, moving plants to protected spots for winter in cold-climates, and periodic repotting. We cover this more thoroughly later in this chapter.

Matching Plants with Pots

Imagine those daylilies brightening up your front porch, their silky trumpets heralding a soft summer breeze — but what kind of pot to show off their multicolor magic?

And how about that gorgeous Asian urn you got at a garage sale. What can you grow in it? Sometimes we start with the plant, and sometimes with the pot — either way can work.

Along with the aesthetics of matching the plant to the right pot, perennials demand that you consider another factor: the plant's size now *and* at maturity. For example, a 4-inch daylily may ultimately spread out to a 2-foot diameter — eventually, you need a very wide pot. But right now, introducing the 4-inch plant to a 24-inch pot doesn't make much sense — especially because you risk making your plant unhappy when all that extra soil creates inhospitably soggy conditions. Remember that in a pot, a perennial may not get quite as big as a ground-grown plant, but it may come close.

So how do you choose the right size pot for now and for later? Two choices: Put that little plant into a 6-inch (or 10-inch) pot and repot it to larger size pots as it grows, or put it in a pot that can accommodate its ultimate size and add annuals to fill the empty space for now (expect them to die before the daylily needs the extra space). Make sure the pot you decide to use is large enough to accommodate the ongoing root growth while remaining topple-free as the plant matures. (We use daylilies as an example here, but the same holds true for any perennial.)

Planting Perennials in Containers

At nurseries and garden centers, you find that perennials are sold mostly in 2-inch, 4-inch, and larger pots, including gallon cans. To plant these, follow the basic steps outlined in Chapter 5. Choose or make a potting mix that matches the perennial's normal soil requirements (if your plant's fussy about such things as acidity and alkalinity); make sure the mix contains plenty of sand or perlite to ensure that it drains quickly.

If you buy perennials by mail order, they're likely to arrive as bare-root plants. The roots are exposed and devoid of any potting soil — a handy, lightweight way to ship perennials and a healthy way to start new plants.

So you may open the box of perennials that came in the mail and find a bunch of small plants with their roots embedded in paper or wood shavings, all loose in a plastic bag. Or you may find what look like only roots. Are they alive? Are they dead? What do you do with them? Here are the basic planting steps:

1. **Remove the plastic wrapping.**

2. **Gently extricate the plant roots from the paper or wood shavings.**

   Alternatively, if the material is biodegradable, just leave it on the roots and plant it with your plant. The wrap protects the roots from unnecessary disturbance.

3. **Soak the plant in room-temperature tap water for an hour or so before you're ready to plant it.**

Mandevilla Red Riding Hood appears near peak bloom atop the corner post of a wall.

Fragrant lemon grass *(Cymbopogon citratus)* adapts readily to life in a pot

A potted dwarf orange tree thrives in a wind-protected corner of this garden.

Good garden scents are provided by rosemary (left) and lemon verbena (right).

Small patios are eligible for container gardens.

Six dwarf yellow marigold plants, two red geraniums, sweet alyssum, and lobelia provide a welcome view from outside and in the home.

An otherwise abandoned
corner of the house is a
good place for container
plants, such as these
impatiens, pansies,
and daisies.

A plant collector's garden
in containers staged for
height on stone blocks.

Choose a patio-type tomato variety and you can grow and

A garden of specimen cactus is safely exhibited in some interesting pots.

Experiment with container gardening to add variety to your garden design.

4. **Prepare your pot.** Be sure to moisten the potting mix thoroughly and let it drain to settle the soil until it feels about as damp as a wrung-out sponge.

5. **Dig out a hole in the potting mix for the plant.** Make the hole an inch or so deeper and wider than the longest root on the plant.

6. **Gently spread the roots so that they fan out in all directions from the base of the plant.**

   Separating the roots may be difficult if the plant has a particularly intertwined system. Just be sure that the roots are not all clumped together beneath the plant.

7. **Carefully fill in the hole with potting mix, covering the roots as you work up to the base of the plant.**

   Add potting mix until the base of the plant is just below the surface of the soil. Do not cover any of the green, growing parts with potting mix.

8. **Firm the mix around the plant and water it well to eliminate any air pockets in the potting mix.**

   Label the plant with its name and the date when you planted it. You may be surprised how interesting and helpful those labels are when you start to collect more than a few plants.

Caring for Perennials in Containers

Perennials, like all good plants, expect their owners to satisfy their special requirements — but these guys, in truth, are not terribly demanding.

The only plants that don't require some care are dead plants.

Flowering perennials share a common goal with all other plants — they live to make more plants. When you see a perennial whose flowers are fading, remember this is a natural process — after it flowers, the plant produces seeds. Your goal, on the other hand, is probably to enjoy the flowers. When the blooms fade, if the plant is still growing strong, you can encourage a new flush of flowers by *deadheading*: Pinch or cut off the fading flowers right where the flower stalks join the stems. After you deadhead, the plant doesn't have to put its energy into setting seed; instead, the plant can concentrate on making more flowers — just what *you* want.

Cutting back

Some plants grow stronger and bloom better after you cut them back. If you cut back leggy stems as much as halfway, they usually come back fuller and bushier with more blooms. Some plants are best cut back in fall, others in spring. Recommendations for cutting back perennials in pots are the same as for perennials in the ground. Check with a local nursery for advice on timing and how much to cut a particular plant back in your area.

Fertilizing

Since perennials and annuals grow differently, you need to fertilize them differently. Annuals have a quick growth spurt and then poop out — they need a fertilizer that's available quickly and over a short time period. Perennials grow more slowly and over a far longer period of time. Hence, they need a fertilizer that lasts longer — the nutrient needs for annuals and perennials are otherwise pretty much the same.

To feed perennials, some gardeners use only slow-release synthetic fertilizers. Others swear by natural products like bonemeal and blood meal. One good strategy for proper nourishment is to mix slow-release fertilizers into potting soil before planting, and supplement weekly with fish emulsion and other natural products during the plant's major growing season; add more slow-release fertilizer as the old runs out.

A rule of thumb for fertilizing perennials in containers: Find out what specific varieties need in your area and feed just a bit more than you'd deliver to the same plants in the ground. The extra food accounts for the loss of nutrients washed out during watering. For more details on fertilizing, see Chapter 11.

Winter care

In cold-winter climate areas, container-grown perennials cannot be left out in the elements — even if the same plants growing in the ground are perfectly hardy. Check locally to find out exactly which plants survive outdoors all year where you live; you'll also learn by trial and error.

Gardeners in cold climates *overwinter* their plants (keep them in a protected spot) to shelter them until milder temperatures of spring arrive. Like everything else gardeners do, each one has a favorite way of overwintering. Here are two:

- Before cold weather strikes, place more tender perennials, in their pots, in an insulated garage or basement where they can lose their leaves and go into a dormant state. Continue to water once a month through winter to be sure they don't wither and die. Move plants back into the garden in spring, after frost danger has passed.

- For hardy perennials, wait until the first hard frost. Then cut foliage back to just a few inches above the soil. Bury each plant, still in its pot, in the middle of your compost or mulch pile, or place in your basement or an insulated garage. When the weather warms, monitor the pots until you see signs of life from the plant stubs. When plants start to grow, move them back to the garden.

Sooner or Later: Repotting

Because perennials tend to grow larger — in some cases *much* larger — than annuals, you may find your plants outgrowing their pots. (Sure signs: roots filling all available soil space, bulging out at the top. An even surer sign: roots bursting the sides of the container.) At times like these, you need to cut back your plants, divide the roots, and repot in the same container or into a larger container.

Some perennials, like coral bells and hostas, spread by underground roots. In pots, they can eventually grow so crowded that they no longer look good or grow well. When your plants enlarge to this size, think about *dividing* the clump. The ideal time to divide a plant is when it's in its most dormant state, which may be in fall or spring, depending on your climate and the particular type of plant.

To divide a perennial:

1. **Ease the plant from the pot.**

2. **Wash off as much soil as possible — you need to be able to see the roots.**

3. **Using a trowel, garden knife, or whatever tool seems to work for you, gently tease apart the root mass into two or more clumps. These clumps are called** *divisions.* **Be sure each division has a healthy set of roots to support it.**

Repot each clump into a new pot using the bare-root potting procedure described earlier in this chapter. You can also plant clumps to give you new plants in the ground. Or share or swap divisions with your friends and neighbors.

Choosing Perennials for Containers

The following popular perennials qualify as good candidates for container gardening. Everything on the list blooms for a fairly long season and is relatively easy to grow. Most of these plants can work alone in containers or can be combined with annuals or other perennials. (Perennials grown as annuals in many parts of the country are listed in Chapter 6.)

✔ **Agapanthus, or lily of the Nile:** This South African native has long, strappy leaves from 1 to 3 feet long. In spring and summer, they send out tall, onionlike clusters of flowers in shades of blue-purple or white. A single aga-panthus easily fills a 24-inch pot and doesn't need divid-ing for 5 or 6 years. It's is a great all-year, easy-to-grow, long-blooming plant in mild climates. It needs overwin-tering (in basementlike conditions) in a cool climate. The dwarf variety, Peter Pan, grows only to 12 inches tall, ideal for smaller containers.

Hardy to zone 8. Provide full sun or part shade. Keep soil moist but not wet. Divide when roots fill up container.

✔ **Alstroemeria or Peruvian lily:** Not a true lily, but just as beautiful and graceful. Intense hybridization has created a myriad of lily-like multicolored flowers: shades of white with pink, pink with white and yellow, lilac and purple, orange-yellow, and many more color combinations. Leafy stems range from 2 to 5 feet tall.

Hardy to zone 8. In mild-winter areas, Peruvian lilies bloom much of the year. In colder-winter areas, bloom season may be May through summer. Provide full sun or part shade (depending on variety), high-quality soil mix, and moderate amounts of water. Roots are rather brittle; when you plant, set fairly deep, with only the top of the root cluster showing. Roots prefer not to be disturbed, so plant in a container with plenty of room to grow.

✔ **Asparagus fern** *(Asparagus densiflorus)***:** Overall effect is long, billowy clouds of green, sometimes studded with red berries. Arching stems 18 to 24 inches long have 1-inch long, flattened leaves that look a bit like needles. This is an asparagus, not a fern, and it's easy and fast-growing in containers — a great choice for baskets, alone or with shade-loving companions.

Hardy to zone 9. Provide full sun or part shade. Keep well-drained soil just barely moist. Overwinter in colder areas of the country. Trim out old, dead branches and repot overcrowded plants or divide old clumps.

✔ **Blanketflower** *(Gaillardia)***:** Tough, native American plants have a ruggedly handsome look with daisylike flowers in beautiful yellows to reds, oranges, and burgundies in different patterns and combinations. Grow 2 to 4 feet tall and spread into a dense mound of blooms.

Hardy to zone 3. Provide full sun, fast-draining soil mix, minimal water. When mature, plants can fill a container completely on their own — don't combine them with other plants in the same container. Cluster pots of blanketflower with other low-growing perennials, separate pots of annuals, or tall grasses.

✔ **Blue marguerite** *(Felicia)***:** Blue daisies with yellow centers are tiny but profuse. Main bloom season is summer, but in frost-free areas expect flowers in winter and early spring — especially if you remove faded flowers. Grow up to 2 feet tall, shrubby and a bit sprawly. This is a tender plant grown as an evergreen perennial in mild climates, but as an annual where winters are cold.

Hardy to zone 9. Provide full sun. Constantly pinch, prune, and groom flowers to contain vigorous growth and control tendency to become a bit raggedy.

✔ **Chrysanthemums:** Familiar autumn flowers make chrysanthemums a garden favorite. So-called florist's chrysanthemum is sold year-round at supermarkets —

typical use is as instant color, then thrown away. But look beyond the florist version to hundreds of other varieties, typically in shades of yellow, white, bronze, and red, in sizes ranging from 6 inches to 4 feet tall. Choose compact varieties for containers. Use taller, more upright types in center of large container plantings.

Hardiness depends on variety. Provide full sun and regular water. Pick fading flowers to prolong the blooms. Divide clumps every few years.

✔ **Coral bells (*Heuchera*):** Flower clusters on stalks as long as 3 feet feature drooping, bell-shaped blooms in shades of red, deep pinks, coral, and white. Foliage is nice, too — long, lobed leaves are green with shades of red and purple. Coral bells are not plants to feature alone in containers, but they combine beautifully with annuals like pansies and other perennials such as hosta.

Hardy to zone 4. Provide full sun in cool climates and part shade where it's hot. Plant groups of coral bells toward the rim of a large pot, next to taller and bushier plants that also require regular water. Plants need to be divided every few years when they start to look woody.

✔ **Coreopsis:** A container of blooming coreopsis can look like golden sunshine on your patio. *Coreopsis grandiflora* grows to 2 feet high and 3 feet wide with 2- to 3-inch bright yellow flowers.

Hardy to zone 3. Provide full sun and fast-draining soil mix. Keep blooms coming by cutting off fading flowers. If there are too many blooms to cut individually, shear back all stems — and expect another round of flowers.

✔ **Daylilies (*Hemerocallis*):** Choose from numerous varieties with flowers in yellow, orange, red, rust, or burgundy — and every imaginable color combination. Blooms rise regally above the leaves and face north, east, south, and west. Better yet, the daylily is an easy plant to grow almost everywhere. Varieties can be either deciduous (better for cold climates) or evergreen. Plants have long, strappy leaves that can grow 2 feet or taller. Dwarf daylilies — a nice choice for containers —typically grow to only 6 or 10 inches tall.

Hardy to zone 4. Daylilies are tough. Provide full sun with a bit of shade in very hot summer areas. Keep soil moist during bloom time. To prolong the flowering season, snap off spent flowers. Plants spread by underground rhizomes and need to be divided every few years — which is easy. If you have a friend who grows daylilies that you admire, ask for a division next time!

✔ **Delphinium:** Thumb through a gardening magazine and you probably come across a picket-fence-enclosed garden planted with elegant blue-flowering delphiniums — the classic, photogenic perennials. Delphiniums grow as tall as 6 feet with stalks of blue, lavender, white, pink, or yellow flowers, mostly in summer. More compact varieties — only 2 to 3 feet tall — work best in containers: Try to find Connecticut Yankee or Blue Fountains.

Delphiniums grow in zones 3–7 and parts of zone 9 with cool night temperatures. Plant in rich, well draining soil mix that's not too acidic. Provide full sun and fertilize regularly. You may need to stake tall flowers.

✔ **Euryops:** This is a landscape and container mainstay in mild climates long blooming and very easy to grow. Shrubby daisy, from 2 to 6 feet tall, blooms heavily in late winter and early spring, then off and on throughout the rest of the year. *Euryops pectinatus* has gray-green leaves. *E. p.* Viridis has deep green leaves.

Hardy to zone 9. Provide full sun. Allow soil to dry out a bit between waterings. After main bloom period, cut plant back by about one-third.

✔ **Foxglove (*Digitalis*):** Usually thought of as a towering background plant, consider the compact varieties for containers: Foxy, Excelsior, and Gloxiniiflora are in the 2- to 3-foot range. Flowers from late spring to early fall are tubular, in shades of purple, white, yellow, with striped and speckled throats.

Hardy to zone 4. Provide full sun or light shade and regular water. A single foxglove can fill a pot 18 inches in diameter. When the flower stalk fades, cut it at the base — you may get a second bloom. These are biennials not perennials, so don't expect year-after-year bloom.

✔ **Hosta, or plantain lily:** This is a great plant for containers in the shade. Grow hosta for its big oval or heart-shaped leaves, in deep green, chartreuse, and many other shades. Plants form mounds from 6 inches to 5 feet tall, depending upon species.

Hardy to zone 4. Hostas go dormant in the winter, requiring overwintering in colder climates. New leaves appear from the roots in early spring. Divide plants when they outgrow their containers.

✔ **Lavender (*Lavandula*):** English, French, and Spanish lavender are just a few types of this fragrant, favorite perennial. Shrublike plants grow 1 to 3 feet tall with slender stalks of purplish flowers at the tips. Lavender is an outstanding container plant — mostly because portability lets you move plants where you can easily snatch a few leaves or flowers and appreciate the fragrance. Dwarf varieties — Compacta and others — work especially well in containers.

Hardy to zone 5, but varies by species. Lavender is evergreen in mild climates and dies back in cold places, where plants can be overwintered. Or start with new plants each year. Provide full sun and well-drained, sandy soil. Let soil dry out between waterings. Lavender works well by itself in pots — its preference for dry conditions makes it incompatible with most other plants. Cut plants way back (halfway or so) after first bloom period.

✔ **Marguerite (*Chrysanthemum frutescens*):** If you are like the rest of us, this may be the first perennial that you grow in a container — very easy, fast growing, long blooming, abundant. White, yellow, cream, or pink daisies bloom continuously over the summer. Shrubby plants grow into a dense mass 4 feet tall.

Hardy to zone 9, can be grown as a summer annual everywhere else. Full sun. To control size and force more blooms, pinch tips right from the beginning. In mild climates, cut back by at least one fourth in early spring.

✔ **Penstemon, or beard tongue:** Penstemons abound in all parts of the U.S. They're shrublike plants, 2 to 5 feet tall, with spikes of tubular flowers in shades of white to coral, pink to red, and purple. Hummingbirds love the flowers. Best bets for containers are *P. gloxinoides* hybrids, with bushy, compact growth. Combine with lower-growing, broad-leafed perennials such as lamb's ear.

Hardiness depends on variety. *P. gloxinoides* can grow year-round only in mild climates; elsewhere treat it like an annual. Provide full sun, unless you live in a very hot climate where plants may need a bit of shade in summer. Keep soil mix very well-drained — too much water and too rich of soil can be deadly. For a strong second bloom, cut off all dead flower spikes.

✔ **Pinks and carnations** *(Dianthus):* This is a huge family, most of them carrying a familiar, wonderfully spicy fragrance — boutonniere-type carnations are the most familiar. For containers, consider compact types: cottage pinks, border carnations, and China pinks. Plants grow 8 to 16 inches tall, covered with a profusion of fragrant flowers in white to pink to magenta.

Hardiness depends on variety; most are hardy to zones 3 or 4. Plant in light, well-drained soils. Provide part shade in hottest summer areas. Water well, but don't overwater. Cut or pinch fading flowers to prolong bloom.

✔ **Primroses:** Their long, crinkly leaves and clusters of flowers in bright shades of blue, yellow, magenta, lavender, and white make them the perfect cottage garden accent. At least 500 different species and varieties, but you can't go wrong with English primrose *(Primula polyantha);* it's easy to grow, one of the first plants to bloom in spring. In the garden, primroses are usually planted at the edge of borders to draw attention to their beautiful flowers. Use that same principle in mixed flower pots, planting primroses at the perimeter of large pots; or fill containers with single colors.

English primroses are hardy to zone 3. Where winters are mild and summers long and hot (such as in California), grow primroses for bloom from fall through early spring. Provide full sun in cool climates (or if grown to bloom in winter), part shade in warm climates. Make sure soil mix is high in peat moss. Keep soil moist.

✔ **Purple fountain grass** *(Pennisetum setaceum Rubrum):* Grasses are strikingly beautiful in pots. This is one of the more striking, forming graceful mounds of purplish-brown leaves up to 2 or even 4 feet tall. In summer, fuzzy pink or purplish flower spikes form. If you prefer to control the spread of grasses throughout your garden, cut off seedheads before they mature.

Hardy to zone 8, but you can grow it as an annual in colder climates. Provide full sun and almost any soil mix. Combine with other perennials that require little water.

✔ **Sage** *(Salvia):* You may think of sage as a culinary herb, but the 900+ types of ornamental sages are plants of tremendous beauty and usefulness in the garden. Perennial salvias tend to be shrublike, ranging from 12 inches to 6 feet tall. Flowers grow on flower spikes, in shades of pink, red, white, coral, blue, and purple. Some salvias stand tall and upright; others cascade. Good choices for containers are mealy blue sage *(S. farinacea),* with foot-long spikes of blue flowers; and cherry sage *(S. greggii),* a low bush that blooms summer through fall.

The two types mentioned are hardy to zone 8. Provide full sun. Pinch frequently, starting when plants are young, to produce bushy growth. Cut plants way back in spring.

✔ **Yarrow *(Achillea):*** Available in many varieties, yarrows are ground-hugging perennials with feathery leaves and delightful flowers in shades ranging from yellow to pink, white to crimson red. Tall stalks are topped with flat clusters of flowers, 2 to 4 inches in diameter. Handsome foliage is green or gray-green, depending upon the variety. Yarrows spread easily by roots; a single 4-inch-pot plant quickly fills a container. Use low-growing, creeping varieties to fill blank spaces and spill over the edges of containers that include taller and bushier perennials. Use taller varieties (up to 3 feet) as the centerpiece of a mixed pot.

Hardy to zone 3. Full sun and minimal water. Divide in spring when the clumps grow too large or too raggedy. Keep overwintering dormant plants on the dry side.

Don't be limited by our list. Nearly any perennial can grow in a container if you're willing to work with it. Here are ten more to consider. (When shopping, remember to look for compact, bushy varieties. Check locally for best growing tips.)

✔ **Artemisia Powis Castle:** Silver foliage plant, sun

✔ **Aster:** Richly colored daisies, sun

✔ **Astilbe:** Spikes of flowers, part shade

✔ **Bellflower *(Campanula):*** Blue flowers for baskets, sun or part shade

✔ **Catmint *(Nepeta):*** Little blue flowers, sun

✔ **Diascia:** Pink, sun

✔ **Erigeron:** Daisies in many colors, sun

✔ **Gazania:** Festive daisies, sun

✔ **Lenten rose *(Helleborus):*** Foliage and blooming plant, shade

✔ **Statice *(Limonium):*** Purple, sun

Chapter 8

Vegetables and Herbs

• •

In This Chapter

▶ The taste pleasures of vegetables in containers

▶ Vegetable needs

▶ Eligible herbs for container gardening

• •

*D*eep red, vine-ripened tomatoes marinate in olive oil with garlic and fresh basil, and the lettuce in the salad bowl is practically still growing — all harvests from your patio. You have to be kidding! Achieving this vision isn't as daunting a task as you may expect. Growing vegetables in containers — for a patio, deck, balcony, or even out in the garden — is not that difficult. And the tasty payoff makes mobile vegetable farming even more rewarding.

With some care and a lot of sun, you can be eating your own container-grown produce all summer long. Apartment dwellers and homeowners alike find container vegetables appealing. First, the convenience is tough to match: Just walk out on the deck and snip some lettuce for a salad or swipe a few peas for a stir-fry. And second, the flexibility yields some fresh ideas: Combining ornamentals and edibles in the garden is a popular design concept these days. You can even move containers from deck to garden and back. With vegetables in containers, you truly can have a movable feast.

And don't overlook herbs for containers. Usually less demanding than vegetables, many perennial culinary herbs are of Mediterranean origin and like it on the hot and dry side. Brush by a pot of thyme, rosemary, or sage on the way to the door and you may imagine you're in the south of France.

What Container Vegetables and Herbs Really Need

If you grow vegetables in the ground, you know that the No. 1 rule is to keep them racing along — with plenty of water, fertilizer, sunlight, and whatever else the specific crops require. Providing the essentials to vegetables and herbs growing in containers can be more challenging because their growing space is limited. To ease caretaking, container plants can grow right outside your back door where you can dote on them. When you know what it needs, your portable garden is likely to reward your attention with tasty returns!

The right container

First question: Are you growing vegetables and herbs for show or just production? If all you want is to pick the produce and you don't care what the container looks like, requirements are pretty basic.

The container must be big enough. A minimum size for most vegetables and herbs is a diameter of 8 inches and depth of 12 inches, but a diameter of 12 to 18 inches and a depth of 15 inches is preferable to accommodate the necessary volume of soil and water. It must have drain holes at the bottom. Vegetables and herbs can thrive in all sorts of containers that meet the size and drainage requirements, but that miss the boat in beauty: leaky buckets, garbage cans with holes, large plastic buckets from delicatessens, and even plastic milk jugs.

If the containers are going to be part of your garden scene, you probably want something more presentable (but with the recommended size and drain holes). Remember that terra-cotta, no matter how attractive, tends to dry out quickly — a major problem for vegetables and herbs racing full steam ahead. You may be better off planting in plastic. If you want a big container to hold a number of vegetables and herbs or a whole salad's fixings, an oak half-barrel is hard to beat.

Soil mix

Commercial soil mixes (see Chapter 4), can be used straight from the bag. But many vegetables and herbs benefit from additional organic matter like bagged compost or ground bark: Add one part of organic matter to three parts soil mix.

Fertilizer

In general, vegetables and herbs are heavy feeders — especially when grown in containers. Nutrient needs vary according to what you're growing. Lettuce and other leafy crops need nitrogen to produce those leaves, whereas tomatoes need some nitrogen to grow, but too much can inhibit flowering — no flowers, no tomatoes.

As a general rule, add an all-purpose dry fertilizer — organic or chemical — according to package directions when you plant. Organic fertilizers release their nutrients slowly; chemical fertilizers release all their nutrients at once, unless you pay a lot more and get the slow-release kind.

As container crops are growing, fertilize regularly, following label directions, and the suggestions for different crops discussed later in this chapter. Most people prefer to use a soluble fertilizer applied as you water. Some gardeners swear by fish emulsion — smelly, but not likely to burn or overfeed.

Water, water, water

Watering is always important with container plants, and it's even more so with vegetables and herbs — let them wilt once and they may never really get back on track. Containers can dry out in a day or in a few hours depending on the planter's size and intensity of the summer heat; rewetting a dry pot may seem impossible. To avoid the problem, check pots and planters often and do not allow the soil to dry out more than an inch or two below the surface.

Experienced tomato growers know that if watering is not consistently maintained, tomato plants are unable to take up calcium, a much-needed nutrient. The result is tomatoes with a dark, leathery spot on the blossom end (the bottom). The telltale coloration doesn't signal a disease, and there's no magic spray to fix it, so pay attention.

Sunlight

Along with watering, sunshine is the other limiting factor in vegetable and herb gardening anywhere. Most vegetables need an minimum of six hours of direct sunlight — that is, sun on the plant, not somewhere nearby. Exceptions are lettuce and spinach, which actually benefit from some shade in the heat of midsummer to keep them from *bolting* — sending up flower heads that end your salad-picking days.

Favorite Vegetables for Containers

Theoretically, you can grow just about any vegetable in a container. Questions do come up, though, about the appropriate pot for those 600-pound pumpkins — maybe the right container is the back of the pickup that hauls the monster to the county contest weigh-in. We suggest that you grow crops that can provide you with at least a few fresh meals and that don't monopolize your whole patio or life.

Try to choose container-friendly varieties, vegetables that are naturally limited in size or that are the results of breeding specifically for potting (lots of vegetables are bred for small spaces, including containers).When you read seed catalogs, look for varieties described with words like these:

- Compact
- Good for containers
- Bush-type
- Baby vegetable
- Midget
- Dwarf
- Tiny
- Teeny-tiny
- Teeny-weeny-tiny

You want to avoid varieties with names like these:

- Jumbo
- Gargantua
- Mammoth
- The Whopper
- Big Bertha
- Big Bopper
- Shaquille

The following vegetables are great choices for moderate-size containers, from 8 to 18 inches in diameter. Plan to plant when you put out ground-grown vegetables in your area. Start with seeds or nursery transplants, and follow the recommendations for spacing provided on seed packets and in vegetable guides.

Beans

Bush varieties like Kentucky Wonder Bush, Jade, and Royal Burgundy stay compact, have high yields, and mature all at once, usually earlier than pole beans. Despite their leggy style, pole varieties such as the standard Blue Lake can do fine in pots as long as you provide stakes or taut strings for them to run up; the effect can be attractive, especially for a balcony. Pick pole beans continually or they stop blooming. Plant bean seeds in spring when it finally gets really warm in your part of the country — as late May in some areas. After seeds sprout, thin seedlings so that they stand 6 inches apart.

Beets

Beets offer a two-for-one treat: You can eat the tops as well as the roots. Plant seeds in early spring or fall in mild-winter climates. For containers, choose smaller varieties like Action or Kestrel.

Cabbage and kinfolk

The Brassicas include broccoli, cabbage, cauliflower, and kale: All need similar care and cool weather. Plant nursery seedlings in early spring or fall in mild-winter climates. Broccoli and kale require less fertilizer than cauliflower and cabbage. Cabbages can grow 10-pound heads — how much coleslaw can you eat? You may want to try the mini-cabbage Dynamo.

Carrots

Carrots need a light soil mix (plenty of sand) to form the roots that we all like to munch. But, do you want to grow a 9-inch-long carrot in an 8-inch deep pot? Think about it. With containers only 8 inches deep, the stubby types like Planet make more sense. Thumbelina is the taste-test queen. Also, give Minicor or Partima a chance to prove themselves.

Corn

Surely not! But yes, a few scaled-down varieties of corn can be grown in deep containers — as long as you don't demand something as high as an elephant's eye. Provide soil mix with lots of organic matter and a deep, large container like a half-barrel (up to 20 seeds planted per barrel). Plan on watering abundantly. Sow seeds in spring when weather warms up. Choose from shorter varieties such as Sugar Buns and Quickie (both extra sweet); popcorn Tom Thumb; and ornamental Wampum or Little Jewels.

Cucumbers

If you choose a vining type of cucumber, like Marketmore or Sweet Success, provide space and a trellis for climbing. Or go with a bushy type: Fanfare or Salad Bush, for example. Cucumbers need hot weather. Sow seeds in spring after the weather warms up.

Eggplant

Warm, rich soil mix and hot sun are the ingredients for successful eggplants. Try Bambino or the eloquently named No.

226. Plant nursery seedlings, one to a pot, after weather warms up in spring.

Lettuce

Reward yourself with green salad early in the year. Lettuce grows quickly, can be planted in cool, spring weather, and harvested within four weeks. Plant seeds or seedlings every few weeks for a constant supply; keep summer plantings in a partly shaded spot. Leaf lettuces (Slobolt, Red Sails, Oak Leaf, Salad Bowl, to name a few) can be harvested the earliest by cutting leaves rather than cutting the whole plant. (Crops that are continually harvested need fertilizing every couple of weeks with a weak solution that's heavy on the nitrogen.) Leaf lettuces can also be cut down whole; if watered and fertilized, they resprout from the base.

Buttercrunch and Tom Thumb are butterhead lettuces: They make small, loose heads that stand up well to hot weather. For gourmet gardeners, mesclun is a mix of greens that are sown together and harvested small; the blend contains interesting textures and flavors, including some hot greens.

Onions

Scallions, green onions, bunching onions — call them what you may, but try to plant some every couple of weeks from early spring to fall for a constant kitchen supply. Don't be concerned about what type; buy a bag of onion sets at the garden store and plant 2 to 3 inches deep.

Peas

Pick from peas for shelling — Maestro, Lincoln, and many others; peas for pea pods like Oregon Sugar Pod II; and snap peas such as Sugar Snap and Sugar Ann. Some are climbers and need support; others are bush types and can, thankfully, be left alone. Plan to sow any variety by April 1 in most climates; fall is a good time to plant in mild-winter areas.

Peppers

Nearly all peppers, even the sweet ones, are a hot item in the garden, and just the right size for containers. Set plants out when the weather turns warm for the season. Colorful sweet peppers include Early Cal Wonder, Northstar, and Jingle Bells. The following are a few hot peppers rated for their temperature, from mild to steam-coming-out-your-ears: Anaheim, Surefire, Riota (particularly good choice for a container), and Habanero.

Potatoes

In March, take a big, plastic trash can (really), poke holes in the bottom and sides, put 10 inches of soil mix in the bottom, then plant potato eyes (hunks of potatoes with growth buds) 1 or 2 inches deep. When the plants sprout, layer straw around the stems to cover all but the top leaves. Continue to fill in with straw as leaves grow taller, water well, and you can expect a can-full of spuds by summer harvest. We're not saying that a trash receptacle is the most attractive container around, but it's certainly a conversation piece and fun for kids. Choose from potato varieties offered at your garden center in the spring or order from a catalog.

Radish

Radishes provide an easy salad ingredient that can be ready to eat just three weeks after the seeds sprout. Go with round types like Easter Egg because they're shallow-rooted.

Spinach

Spinach comes in several main types: smooth-leafed varieties like Mazurka, Olympia, and Hector; crinkle-leafed savoy types such as Bloomsdale Savoy; and the semi-savoyed types like Tyee and Italian Summer. Each variety produces delicious greens for salads or light steaming. Many varieties, such as Tyee, overwinter well in milder climates.

Squash

Summer squash plants can be bullies, taking over the garden. Even varieties described as compact, such as Spacemiser or yellow Gold Rush, can fill a half barrel — one plant is enough. Trade your squash plantings with gardener friends. You can wind up with a much more colorful pot of ratatouille. Plant seeds or nursery transplants in spring after the weather has warmed up.

Swiss chard

Easy to grow, but watch the size — no more than three plants, even for a large container. Plant in early spring. Good bets for containers are Fordhook Giant and Rhubarb (with red stems).

Tomatoes

You have to try at least one tomato in a container just for the fun of observing it up close. And even if you get only a few fresh tomatoes fruits, you're assured that they taste better than those pink, mealy objects found in grocery stores most of the year. Tomato plants are classified as either determinate (those that grow to a point and stop) or indeterminate (those that have yearnings to take over your entire living space). Either type needs some sort of support — cage, trellis, or stake and twine.

Delicious and prolific cherry tomatoes include Sweet Million and Yellow Pear (both indeterminate), and Sun Gold (determinate). Some cherries (Patio or Micro-Tom) are small enough for a hanging basket. Determinates that slice up well include Oregon Spring, Celebrity, and Santiam. Indeterminate slicers are Stuplce, Big Beef, and Early Cascade.

Tomatoes need a deep container. Plant nursery seedlings in spring after weather has warmed up. Bury the seedlings past the bottom sets of leaves (after removing the leaves); the stem develops roots along the buried part. Plan on conscientious watering and fertilizing.

Herbs in Containers

Herbs make perfect sense for containers. Most of them look good as they grow. And you want them handy to the kitchen or patio. Who's in favor of jogging out past the pumphouse to the back 40 when you desperately need rosemary for the chicken you're barbecuing?

Most herbs are easy to grow. Commercial soil mix is fine. Many herbs prefer conditions on the dry side because they are used to spartan conditions in nature. Regular feeding once or twice a month can be a big help.

Planting herbs is simple: Space out seedlings in your container and fill the gaps with soil, as shown in Figure 8-1.

Figure 8-1: Planting herbs couldn't be easier. _____

Here's a selection of herbs to tuck into almost any pot in full sun:

Basil

Basil is an annual that needs hot weather to grow. Plant seed or transplants when you're sure that the overnight temperature is not below 50°F, and expect to be rewarded with fast-growing plants and lots of pesto by summer. Fertilize moderately with nitrogen. Many types are available (cinnamon, Thai, lemon, globe); all do well in pots.

Chives

Growing from bulbs, this onion-family member begins growth in early spring and is hardy to zone 3. Snip and use the leaves. Keep plants outside (dormant) over the winter or bring them inside, place in a sunny window, and continue to snip and use. During the growing season, cut down plant completely once or twice and fertilize with nitrogen. Chive blossoms are edible, and the lavender color gives a nice tint to herb vinegars.

Oregano

This herb is easy to grow in pots, although it still develops long, lanky branches; don't be afraid to cut them back. Use the leaves fresh or dried.

Parsley

Choose between curly-leafed and flat-leafed (sometimes called Italian) — both pretty, bright green plants. Parsley is biennial, growing one year, and then flowering and setting seed the next. Sow seeds every spring (even though sprouting is slow) or start with nursery transplants. Parsley has a long taproot, so be sure to use a container at least 12 inches deep. Part shade is best.

Rosemary

A shrub in its native habitat, rosemary requires a large container with a well-drained soil mix (even a cactus mix) and hot sun. Rosemary is not reliably hardy below zone 8, but small plants may overwinter indoors with bright sunlight.

Sage

More cold-hardy than rosemary, sage can survive outside to zone 4. Sage is available in many varieties: tricolor, purple, golden, and dwarf — a good bet for a container.

Savory

With a strong peppery aroma, winter savory is a wonderful addition to a pot of beans. It's hardy to zone 6. Summer savory is an annual with a more delicate aroma.

Tarragon

An ungainly plant, tarragon belongs in a pot with more orderly herbs (such as sage). It's hardy to zone 4.

Thyme

Varieties abound, but don't pass up common thyme for any kind of cooking. Hardy to zone 5, thyme likes dry conditions and lots of sun. Special culinary thymes include lemon and silver.

Chapter 9

Cactus and Succulents

· ·

In This Chapter

▶ Sizing up the succulent family

▶ Finding your plant's place in the sun

▶ Picking a suitable container home

▶ Tending to long-term needs

▶ Picking your prickly friends wisely

· ·

*T*here's nothing more pleasing than a pot full of cactus to remind us of dry, warm places where we want to be — unless it's a margarita, but see how long that lasts on a sunny patio. Cactus and succulents (we're lumping them together) have many other virtues when grown in containers. Here are a few:

  ✔ Cactus and succulents offer advantages to gardeners who may not have all the time in the world. They usually require far less maintenance than, say, a pot of pansies.

  ✔ They offer surprising contrasts in the garden or on the patio — instead of flower color, we're talking about shapes that range from bulbous to stringy, and textures from smooth to spiny to hairy.

  ✔ Most cactus and succulents grow slowly, and that means less time repotting plants that outgrow their containers. Of course, slow growth may also mean waiting a few years (how about 30?) before you're bowled over by the extraordinary blooms some cactus produce.

  ✔ Most important for gardeners north of zone 9: Containers let you move plants indoors when the temperature drops. Actually quite a few cactus and succulents can be grown outdoors, far from the desert — hens and chicks, prickly pear — and others can winter in an indoor

window seat. You may want to build one of those huge
Victorian conservatories to house their succulent
collections.

Rules of the Game

A succulent is a plant that has adapted to arid conditions by
creating water storage units in leaves, stems, and roots.
Succulents are native to many different environments: deserts
that may suffer slightly cool temperatures at night (50s); high
deserts that may get snow or frost; seaside areas where water-
holding capacity has more to do with protection from high
salinity than the dryness of the surroundings; dry, cold moun-
tainside crevices; and many temperate areas.

Most succulents have evolved to store water during the rainy
season, and then use it during the dry season. Some succulents rely on summer rains, but for many, the wet season
arrives in winter, and that's when growth occurs. The rest of
the year, lying dormant, the plants hunker down and wait. As
you may know from visits or pictures, the Southwest desert in
spring is a sight to behold: Winter rains come and suddenly
cactus everywhere are adorned in bright bursts of flowers.

Cactus are a type of succulent, set apart from other of the
fleshy-tissued plants by two features: One is that cactus have
a structure called an *areole* at the growing point, sometimes
visible as small pads. This is where new leaves, stems, and
flowers spring up. Also, most cactus have spines, which
makes them interesting to look at, and especially amusing to
handle. In this chapter when we refer to succulents, we mean
to include cactus as well, unless we say otherwise. And while
we're discussing really important matters, we better get this
right out in the open: We use *cactus,* not cacti or cactuses, as
the plural of cactus. *Webster's* blesses cactus as the third-
choice plural, and we think it sounds better.

Growing Cactus/Succulents in Containers

Light and temperature are the defining needs of many succulents. In general, most need a great deal of bright light, although some take part shade. Most cannot survive for more than a night with temperatures below 40°F, but some are hardy in all climates. Looking on the bright side (so to speak), the range of preferences means that there are succulents for every garden taste and climate.

The basic rules for growing succulents in containers:

- ✔ Provide as much light as possible during the summer — although full sun in really warm places, including their desert homelands, can be too hot for many succulents in the confines of a container. Some types prefer part shade — see the list at the end of this chapter.

- ✔ Protect succulents from cold weather in the winter. Move them indoors to a sunny window where temperatures do not drop below 40°F.

If you have large heavy containers, plan to put them on wheels — or start pumping iron.

Choosing containers

Succulents lend themselves to terra-cotta pots — the attraction is probably the desert look about both plants and the containers. Terra-cotta also is porous, which keeps roots from sitting in water; stone and concrete pots also work well.

Making sure the container has drainage holes is another important rule — sometimes so obvious it may be missed. Feel free to use a shallow container (4 to 6 inches deep) if it looks best for your plants — succulent roots don't go very deep. For a plant with a rounded shape, choose a container that's 2 inches wider than the plant. For an upright plant, choose a pot that's half the diameter of the plant's height.

When we select containers, cactus and succulents sometimes bring out the eccentric in us. We've seen small hens and chicks or other rosette-forming succulents planted in strawberry jars, old boots, or even worn-out tennis shoes.

Another popular choice is *hypertufa* — a do-it-yourself project made with concrete, peat moss, and the mold of your choice. Hypertufa's rugged beauty is nice for ornamental succulents like sedum, echeveria, and sempervivum.

Selecting soil mix

Quick drainage is the most important quality of a soil mix designed for succulents. The standard mix consists of one-half organic matter (peat moss, leaf mold, or something like that) and one-half grit (crushed rock or sand). You can find many cactus and succulent mixes already bagged.

Planting

Design your succulent containers following the same principles that you apply for other plants: combining something tall and spiky, something mounded, something trailing. A well-balanced landscape can be accomplished by using one large container with several plants. Or put each plant in its own container and then group the pots — this mix-and-match method gives you freedom to rearrange on a whim.

When planting cactus, care is the key word — for yourself and the plant. Wear thick gloves and/or wrap the cactus in a sleeve of thickly layered paper and use the ends as a handle. (If you get stuck with a few spines, use cellophane tape to remove them.)

1. **Cover the drain hole, as described in Chapter 5.**

2. **Fill the container part way with soil mix and ease the plant into the container, as in Figure 9-1.**

Figure 9-1: With some soil already in the container, carefully set the cactus in.

3. **Use a narrow trowel or spoon to fill around the cactus with soil mix (see Figure 9-2).**

   Most cactus and many other succulents have shallow roots, so do not plant too deeply. Burying part of the stem invites rot to set in. Make sure the soil level is no higher than it was in the plant's nursery container.

4. **Add a top layer of gravel or crushed stone, as in Figure 9-3, to provide a finished, desert-like look that also helps keep the base of the plant dry.**

Buy any bag of gravel you like or choose crushed rock that enhances the look of the plant and the container — something with a pinkish tone, for example, may look nice with terra-cotta. Feel free to add any decorative details at this point — miniature steer skulls, prospector skeletons, and so on.

Figure 9-2: Fill the container with soil mix.

Figure 9-3: For a final touch, add some gravel.

Maintenance

First of all, forget some of the myths that you may have heard or imagined about cactus and succulents. You do need to water them and feed them.

Water regularly during the growing season — remember that this can be winter for some species. Thorough watering is better than a sprinkle every day or two. When the soil is completely dry, it's time to water again. One effective way to water smaller pots is to sit them in water nearly up to their rims and leave them there until the top layer of soil is moist.

During their dormant season and in cool temperatures (50°F), most cactus and succulents can go without water for weeks at a time. Just don't forget about the poor things. Resume regular watering just before the growing season begins.

When plants are in a growing stage, fertilize about once a month — or every other time you water, if you water every two weeks. Succulents need all the nutrients that other plants do — nitrogen, phosphorus, and potassium — plus trace elements. You can use just about any complete liquid fertilizer or a special fertilizer designed for cactus and succulents; or try a tomato fertilizer at half-strength. For more on fertilizing, check Chapter 11.

If you need to repot a cactus, use a piece of rolled-up cloth or paper to remove the plant from its original container, as shown in Figure 9-4.

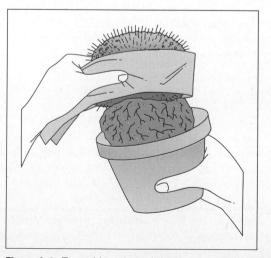

Figure 9-4: To avoid getting pricked, use a rolled-up cloth to remove a cactus from its container.

Which Cactus and Succulents?

Mail-order sources offer tantalizing pictures and descriptions. As with any plant purchase, read carefully and plan ahead. If you live in a cold-winter area, remember to keep in mind what happens to those beauties in January. Buying cactus and succulents locally is always possible — check out nearby nurseries to get a feel for what different plants look like and which are adapted to your climate.

As you shop, look for plants that aren't wrinkled or shrunken at the base near the soil. Avoid cactus with broken spines.

Because succulents come from many different parts of the world with different altitudes, temperature ranges, and rainfall patterns, it's impossible to make blanket statements about which plants to choose and how to care for them. Pay attention to the cultural information for each species, then group the plants in containers accordingly.

Here are just a few of the hundreds of cactus and succulents to look for and try in containers. The plants are listed alphabetically by common name, with the botanical name given to avoid possible confusion. Most are hardy outdoors in zones 9 and 10; in other climates, plan to move the pots indoors for winter. Remember that hardiness zones, when listed, are for plants growing in the ground, and container plants are not that tolerant of cold.

Cactus for containers

You may enjoy growing any of these cactus:

- ✔ *Acanthocalycium glaucum:* Moderate-growing, small grayish mound with brown to black spines has showy yellow or orange flowers. Give it part shade in really hot areas; water in spring and summer.

- ✔ Beehive cactus *(Coryphantha missouriensis):* Native to Canada and the United States, this is a true cold-hardy species, able to grow as far north as zone 3. Only 3 inches tall, the beehive forms clusters with gray spines. Flowers are fragrant and green, followed by red fruit in summer. During the dormant season, beehive cactus may actually shrink so much that it retreats underground. *C. vivipara* is a cold-hardy relative with magenta flowers.

✔ **Bishop's cap or bishop's miter** *(Astrophytum myriostigma):* Short and rotund, its white speckles (rudimentary spines) give it a silvery look. Expect it to grow to the size of a large grapefruit by ten years of age.

✔ **Golden barrel cactus** *(Echinocactus grusonii):* A globe with golden-yellow spines, it grows slowly to 6 inches, sometimes larger. Don't hold your breath waiting for flowers — they appear after 30 or 40 years. Full sun.

✔ **Hedgehog cactus** *(Echinocereus viridiflorus):* Stems form clusters to 6 inches. Flowers are fragrant and lime-green. *E. triglochiodiatus*, a hardier species (to zone 5), has stem clusters to 1 foot, 1-inch pale gray spines, and deep pink flowers.

✔ **Old-man-of-the-mountains** *(Borzicactus celsianus,* **also listed as** *Oreocereus celsianus):* White hairs create a shaggy beard look. The plant forms a medium-size column eventually reaching a foot tall, with magenta flowers popping out here and there.

✔ **Orchid cactus** *(Epiphyllum):* Excellent hanging basket plant, orchid cactus resembles a wad of stems, but in bloom can be spectacular — fragrant flowers in neon colors. Provide part to full shade.

✔ *Parodia:* Globular plants to 1 foot tall grow by forming offsets. Flowers look like daisies. Don't water in winter. Try *P.magnifica* (*P. notocactus*), with white-spined ribs.

✔ **Pincushion cactus** *(Mammillaria bombycina):* Short cylinders up to a foot tall produce offsets covered in soft, white down and yellow spines. Pink flowers are big — at least 3 inches wide.

✔ **Prickly pear or cholla** *(Opuntia):* Prickly pear has flattened, oval stems, and cholla has cylindrical stems. Some are spinier than others. They tolerate rainfall well. Try *O. compressa, O. fragilis,* or *O. vivipara.*

✔ **Sea urchin** *(Echinopsis):* This is a big group of globular or columnar, medium-to-fast-growing plants. Expect a wide choice of flower colors.

Succulents for containers

These are our favorite succulents.

- **Cub's paws *(Cotyledon tomentosa):*** This is a shrubby, spreading, little plant, about a foot high. Deciduous green leaves are toothed at the top and have a reddish margin. Provide part shade.

- ***Crassula pubescens:*** Tuck this small, creeping ground cover into a container. Give it plenty of sun to bring out the leaves' bright red tones.

- ***Echeveria:*** Choose from several species of rosette-forming plants with colorful foliage.

- **Houseleeks or hens and chicks *(Sempervivum):*** These rosette-forming plants are probably the best known succulents. They're available with leaves in shades of green and red — cobweb-looking hairs circle some of the leaves. Plants spread by offsets; if one breaks off, tuck it into another pot, and it will root easily.

- **Jade plant *(Crassula):*** In mild climates, this shiny-leafed favorite can grow up to 6 feet tall and produces little pink flowers in midwinter.

- ***Jovibarba heuffelii:*** Tuck these rosettes into fast-draining pots. Many varieties with leaves of different colors — bronze, chocolate, violet. Hardy to zone 6.

- ***Lewisia rediviva:*** Native to the Rocky Mountains (and hardy to zone 4), this is a colorfully blooming plant that demands very fast drainage. *L. tweedyi*, native to the Cascade Mountains, is hardy to zone 5.

- **Queen Victoria century plant *(Agave victoria-reginae):*** Spiky short-green leaves edged in white form a dramatic 1-foot rosette. Plant is slow growing, and 13-foot (!) flower stalks take 30 years to bloom — not a century. *A. utahensis* is a cold-hardy relative.

- **Sedum:** Among the more versatile container plants. Check hardiness — certain varieties can grow in climates as cold as zone 3. Some form very showy flower heads; a popular choice is *S. spectabile* Autumn Joy.

Chapter 10

Thirst Quenching

You have to admit that our advice so far has been pretty laid-back: Choose terra-cotta or plastic pots, try impatiens or delphiniums, whatever. But when it comes to watering container plants, we are hard-liners. Do it the right way or get out of the game.

Unlike plants growing in the ground that can rely on deep roots to get them through dry spells, container-grown plants have limited soil from which to draw. When they dry out, they really dry out. And the repercussions of becoming parched are usually more severe and permanent than if the plants were in the ground.

What it comes down to is this: If you want to be successful growing plants in containers, that is, if you want your flowers to bloom well and your fruit, herbs, and vegetables to produce a bountiful harvest, you're going to have to become an attentive and efficient waterer. And in this chapter, we show you how.

Why and When Containers Need Water

How often container plants need water and how much they need when they need it depends on several factors, which the next sections cover.

Climate

If you live in an area like Seattle, Washington, or Biloxi, Mississippi, where rainfall is regular and reliable, watering isn't a constant chore, except in prolonged dry spells or periods of drought.

In drier, hotter areas like Los Angeles, California, and Phoenix, Arizona, watering container plants is something that has to be in squeezed into your schedule almost on a daily basis.

Weather

Climate is determined by the average weather where you live on a season-to-season, year-to-year basis. Weather is what's happening outside right now. Out-of-the-ordinary weather can wreak havoc on your plants. Hot, dry winds can dry out a plant growing in a hanging basket or a clay pot, literally, in a matter of minutes.

Table 10-1, in a nutshell, tells you how to adjust watering according to weather conditions. Forgive us if our little chart is too commonsensical:

Table 10-1	Watering According to Weather
Water Less	*Water More*
Cooler temperatures	Warmer temperatures
Cloudy or overcast	Bright sunshine
Low wind	High wind
High humidity	Low humidity
Rain	No rain

Pot type

The porosity of a container influences how much water evaporates through its sides. And that can be a lot. At one extreme are hanging baskets lined with sphagnum moss, which seem to dry out as soon as you turn your back on them in hot weather.

At the other end of the spectrum are plastic pots, metal, or thick concrete containers that hardly lose any moisture through their sides. In the middle are unglazed clay pots, which are pretty porous and dry out quickly, and wooden containers, which dry out slower but, depending on their thickness, tend to lose water through their sides.

Pot color

Lighter-colored containers reflect more sunlight and dry out more slowly than darker-colored ones that absorb heat.

Rootboundedness

Is that a word?

Even if it isn't, the term means a lot to anyone who grows plants in pots. As a plant grows in a container, the roots become more and more crowded. At first, the roots of a recent transplant may not even fill the pot, so the plant's drinking system may not be able get to all the water in the soil. Over time, the roots fill the container and the rootball (roots and soil) becomes a tight mass of roots, especially on larger plants. The rootball then becomes hard to wet, making more frequent waterings necessary.

So, in summary, here are the high points of Watering 101: Just after planting a new container, you have to water it carefully until the roots start to fill the pot. Then you go through a period when you can back off a bit because the roots have a larger soil reservoir to drawn from. But then (all good things must come to an end), as roots start to fill the pot and become rootbound, you have to start watering more often again. Or you could transplant into a large pot.

Soil variations

Most potting soils used for containers are lightweight and dry out fairly quickly. But some dry out faster than others. For example, potting soils that are higher in organic materials like peat moss or compost can hold more water than those that contain a higher percentage of mineral components like sand or perlite. More about potting soils in Chapter 4.

Location, location, location

Containers placed in full sun almost always need more frequent watering than those in shady areas. That's pretty obvious, but things can be more subtle. For example, containers situated on a hot surface like a concrete patio are likely to dry out faster than those on a wood deck, which tends to stay cooler.

Genetic disposition

Most plants grown in containers need consistent soil moisture to grow well. But some plants can go drier than others. For example, let a pot full of lettuce go dry and the leaves lose moisture and probably never completely recover — you may as well replant.

Cactus and succulents, on the other hand, are a lot more forgiving and can go through dry spells quite well; in fact, most prefer to be on the dry side. If they stay too wet, many cactus and succulents rot. Lavender is another plant that does best if soil goes a bit dry between waterings.

You have to remember that some things are beyond your control, but these contributing factors still affect your watering practices. Just go with the flow and make adjustments when and where you can.

Ways to Water Container Plants

Some methods for watering container plants are better than others, but making choices often depends on how many containers you have.

In some areas, certain watering techniques become a matter of necessity rather than practicality. Where droughts are common or water supplies are unpredictable, conservation is the order of the day. You need to water in ways that respects every precious drop. Where foliage diseases like powdery mildew are common, you want to keep water off the plant leaves and apply it to just the roots.

The next few pages describe several fundamental ways to water containers.

Hand watering

Probably the most commonly used method, hand watering allows you to easily make adjustments in how much water each pot gets according to its size and specific needs.

Indoors, it's generally easiest to use one of many handheld watering cans, but there are also little hose setups that can be hooked to the sink faucet. Outdoors, most gardeners find it convenient to drag a hose around to water their pots.

Many excellent types of hose-end attachments let you turn the water on and off without going all the way back to the faucet. Bubbler attachments soften the output of the water, which can prevent washing soil mix out of the container. There are even extensions that make it easier to water hanging pots (see Figure 10-1). Whatever you do, don't let the hose run so forcefully into the container that it washes out soil; soften the water stream with your hand, at least.

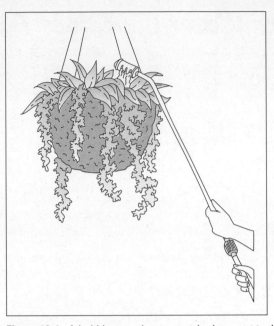

Figure 10-1: A bubbler on a hose extender is a neat tool for watering plants in hanging baskets.

Sprinklers

Although hose-end sprinklers are available in a variety of styles, they're not very efficient for watering containers — just too much water wasted. In a pinch, you may set up a sprinkler to water a raised bed or a grouping of containers, but if that becomes a habit, you're better off putting in a drip system, as described in the next section.

There is one possible problem with overhead watering, whether from a hose, watering can, or sprinkler. In humid climates, overhead watering can spread disease and turn your flowers into a moldy mess. In such areas, either install a drip system or hold the hose or watering can spout right above the rim of the pot so that the water doesn't get on the foliage or flowers.

Drip irrigation

Drip irrigation is a very effective and efficient way to water containers. A drip system provides water slowly through holes or emitters in black plastic pipe. Connect the pipe to a water supply, filter, and often a pressure regulator, and then weave it out (in constantly smaller pipes) to your containers. Water is slowly applied (or dripped) directly to the plants, as shown in Figure 10-2.

Emitters differ by how much water they put out per minute: one-half gallon an hour, 1 gallon per hour, and so on. Drip systems usually have to run at least several hours to wet a large area, such as a raised bed. Smaller pots may only need to be run for an hour, depending on the output of the emitter. Larger pots may need more than one emitter. Watch your system carefully the first few times that you water. Poke around in the soil to see how long you need to water to wet a container, or how long it takes before water runs out the drainage holes. Then make adjustments.

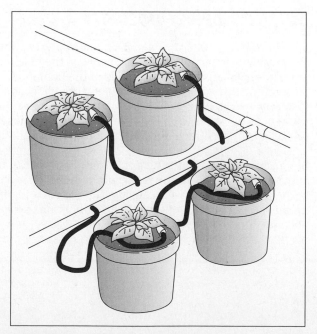

Figure 10-2: A drip irrigation system.

Drip irrigation systems are sold in most nurseries. You can also purchase them through the mail. Pressure-compensating emitters apply water consistently from one end of the line to the other regardless of pressure changes due to uneven ground.

Leaky pipe hoses (sometimes called soaker hoses, which are made of recycled tires) release water along their entire length. If the ground goes up and down at all, they apply water unevenly, but can still be useful in a level raised bed.

Drip irrigation systems hooked to automatic timers can really relieve the chore of watering a lot of containers. And although you may be hard-pressed to imagine weaving plastic pipe all over your porch or patio without creating a messy nightmare, rest assured that all it takes is a little creative thinking, burying some pipe, or running pipe above your plants, along eaves.

If you live in an area where the soil freezes, don't leave your drip system outside in winter. Your pipes may burst. Instead, drain out the water, roll up the pipe, and store it in the garage.

Self-watering pots

Best suited for smaller house plants, self-watering pots are also available in larger versions. Basically, they include a water reservoir, usually in the walls of the container, which is connected to the rootball of the plant through a small wick (like they use in Tiki torches). As the rootball dries out, the wick sucks up water from the reservoir and supplies it to the rootball, keeping it nice and wet (see Figure 10-3).

Be careful with self-watering pots. You don't want to forget about them and not fill the reservoir on time. They can also keep some plants too wet, causing them to rot and die. And because there's no way to leach the salts from a self-watering pot, salt burn can develop.

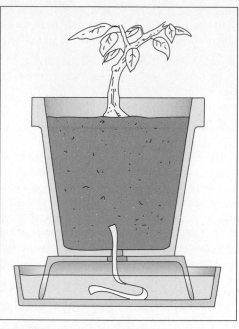

Figure 10-3: A self-watering pot.

How Often Should You Water?

You know that a plant's water needs vary with the weather and the seasons — less in cool weather, more in warm weather, and so on. Even an automated system requires adjustment so that it waters less in spring and more in summer. Plan to practice your powers of observation and make watering adjustments accordingly.

However, there are other ways to tell when your plants need water or when containers are getting dry:

✔ **Your plants can send you a message.** That's right. When plants start to dry out, the leaves droop and wilt. The plant may also lose its bright green color and start to look a little drab. Make your goal to water before a plant reaches that point (consider it a cry for help).

✔ **Dig in the ground.** Stick your finger an inch or two into the soil in the top of a pot. If the soil feels dry, it's close to watering time.

✔ **Lift the pot.** As a pot dries out, it gets lighter. Compare how heavy a pot is right after watering thoroughly with how it feels a few days later. By simply tilting a pot on its edge and judging its weight, you eventually figure out how to tell when it's dry or getting close to it.

✔ **Use a moisture sensor.** Your nursery sells various devices for reading soil moisture. Most have a long, needlelike rod connected to a meter. You push the rod into the soil, and the meter tells you how wet the soil is. These sensors can be pretty handy, but don't trust them too much right off the bat. Some can be thrown off by salts in the soil. To start, see how their readings compare to what you discover by feeling the soil and lifting the pot. Then make adjustments.

Eventually, through observation, digging and lifting, you start to develop a watering schedule and a lot of the guesswork disappears.

How Much Should You Water?

When you water a container plant, the goal is to wet the entire rootball and apply just enough water so that some drains out the bottom. Now, if the container is properly planted, there's space between the top of the soil and container rim that you can fill with water. It may be anywhere from 1 inch in small containers to 4 or 5 inches in larger ones. But whatever the case, you have to fill it more than once to get enough water to wet the rootball. That means, you fill the pot once, let the water soak in, then fill it again, and, if necessary, fill it with water again until the whole rootball is wet and heavy.

This whole soaking thing is a bit tricky for one reason. As the rootball in a container dries, it shrinks, usually pulling away from the edges of the pot. So when you water that first time, the water drains down the edges without wetting the rootball hardly at all.

This phenomenon explains why you need to make several passes with the hose or watering can — so that the rootball swells up a bit and seals the edges of the container, at which point the water can soak in. This is also why you can never judge how wet a rootball is by the amount of water that comes out the drainage hole. You can get fooled every time. Check water penetration by lifting the edge of the pot, as described earlier.

You can wet shrunken rootballs or plants that are really root-bound in a few other ways:

✔ **Water from the bottom.** If you place small trays or saucers underneath your pots to catch excess water, that water is gradually reabsorbed by a dry rootball. You're basically watering from the bottom and at a pace dictated by the plant.

 Its not a good idea to have a container sitting in water for a long time. The rootball becomes too wet and eventually the plant drowns. But submerging a pot partially, or even completely, for just a little while won't hurt and is a great way to wet a really dry rootball.

 In fact, if your houseplants get too dry, just fill up the kitchen sink with water and let the pots bathe for an hour or so, then drain the water. You see that the rootballs are wet.

✔ **Use drip irrigation.** Drip emitters apply water at a slow, steady rate and do a great job of thoroughly wetting the rootball.

Water-Saving Ways

Water shortages are a reality in almost any climate or region. And container plants use a lot of water, more than the same plants in the ground.

Here are a few things that you can do when water is scarce or limited, when you just want to conserve the precious resource of fresh water, or if you just want to ease your watering chores:

✔ **Install drip irrigation.** It applies water slowly without runoff. Drip is definitely the most frugal watering system that you can use.

✔ **Double pot.** If you take a small pot and put it in a bigger pot, you reduce the amount of sunlight that hits the sides of the smaller pot, which helps cool the soil. Cooler soil means less water used.

✔ **Use soil polymers.** Soil polymers are weird Jell-O-like materials that hold hundreds of times their weight in water. If you mix them dry with your soil before you plant, you can stretch the time between waterings.

✔ **Transplant.** Moving a rootbound plant into a bigger container, where it has more soil to draw water from, can greatly reduce your watering chores. Better yet, if a container plant is really too much trouble to water, maybe you're better off planting it in the ground.

✔ **Move pots into the shade.** If the weather really gets hot, move your pots into the shade to cool them down and reduce water use. A few days of less sun won't hurt them.

✔ **Group pots.** If you put pots close together, they can shade each other and reduce the amount of sun that hits their sides.

✔ **Bury the pots.** Huh? That's right, just dig a hole and bury the pots just deep enough so that the rims are covered. Or you can build a wooden box, put the pots in, and fill around the edges with potting soil or organic material like peat moss or ground bark. You still have to water, but you use a lot less, especially if you also wet the soil around the pots. This method is drastic, but if water is really tight, or if you're going out of town for a while, it works.

✔ **Mulch.** A mulch is a layer of organic matter that's spread over the root zone beneath a plant. Several inches of heavy mulch, like large pieces of bark (so that they don't float away when you water) or other material, can cool the soil and reduce evaporation, thus saving water.

✔ **Pull weeds.** Weeds steal water meant for container plants. So keep them pulled.

✔ **Water efficiently.** Do as we suggested earlier in this chapter, and wet the entire rootball. You can have happier and healthier plants, and use less water in the long run.

✔ **Use rainwater.** Put a barrel or other collector where the drain pipes from your roof empty. Then use that water on your flowers.

✔ **Measure rainfall.** Keep track of how much rain you get. An inch is usually enough to let you skip a watering.

✔ **Plant unthirsty plants.** Some cactus and succulents can get by on little water, even when grown in containers.

Who Waters When You're out of Town?

So you're going on vacation and can't find anyone to water your plants. What are you going to do? Start by considering some of the water-saving methods described in the previous section, especially burying the pots or setting up a drip system with an automatic timer. But there are a couple other things you can do.

Wick water

Choosing to wick water is kind of like building your own self-watering pot. It works best on smaller containers, especially houseplants.

Go to a hardware store and buy some long wicks used for Tiki torches (for really small pots, you can use thick cotton string). Wet the wick and use a pencil to push it a few inches into the wet rootball of the plant. Stick the other end in a bowl or glass of water. As the rootball dries, it sucks water from the bowl through the wick, keeping it wet.

Don't try this the day you're getting ready to leave. Set it up a week in advance, to make sure it works, and to see how much of a water reservoir you need. If you use a big bucket to hold the water, you can water several plants at once.

Use soil polymers

Buy some soil polymers (we told you about those a few paragraphs back) at your local nursery, put some in a small plastic cup, and add water to turn them to Jell-O. Turn the cup upside down on top of the soil in your pot. Over time, the polymers slowly release their moisture to water the plant. Again, don't wait to try this on the day you decide to leave. Test it a week or so before you go away to see how fast the water is released and how much polymer you need to use.

You may be able to buy a product that already has ready-to-use, hydrated polymers in a cup. You just flip it over on top of the soil in your pot. See if your nursery has it in stock.

Other Container Watering Tips

To sum up this whole watering business, here are some things not to forget:

- ✔ **Make sure your pots have drainage holes.** Without them, the plant drowns.

- ✔ **Check drainage.** Even if your containers have holes in the bottom, they may fill up with roots, preventing proper drainage. Check the holes occasionally, and cut them open with a knife if necessary.

- ✔ **Use catch trays or saucers.** They help prevent water from getting all over the place when you water houseplants and give any plant a chance to suck up water from below. Remember, though, that the pot isn't happy sitting in water for more than a day or so — the roots drown. If necessary, raise the bottom of the pot out of the tray by placing it on small pieces of wood or bricks.

Chapter 11

Feeding

● ●

In This Chapter

▶ Nourishing your plants for healthy growth

▶ Scoring comprehension in chemistry

▶ Shopping smart with fertilizer lingo

▶ Growing with organic fertilizers

● ●

*T*hinking of your container plants as pets is understandable — after all, plants and pets are living things that provide you with amusement, companionship, and even an occasional gift of shedding (fortunately, hair balls aren't important to this discussion). In return for what your pets/plants do for you, you have certain obligations, with feeding right near the top. Your plants depend on you in much the same way that your Border collie Max does. Generations ago, Max lost the ability to go out and forage for himself. Likewise, container plants can't send roots down deep and wide in the ground as do garden plants. Plants grown in the cushy but confined environment that you create for them search for nutrients within their own boundaries.

We promise to drop the pet metaphor before you start barking back, but not before we stress the importance of properly feeding container plants. You're the caretaker who provides your container plants the right nutrients at the right time. If you don't, you know what can happen. You may be the first to hear from the SPCCP (Society for Prevention of Cruelty to Container Plants).

As you discover in this chapter, different plants need different feeding. Read about special demands in the chapters devoted to types of plants (annuals, cactus, shrubs, and so on). Most importantly, find out why plants need nutrients — and how you can fill those requirements.

Preparing a Good Diet — Plant-Wise

For healthy growth, plants need 16 different elements. Carbon, hydrogen, and oxygen — the foundation blocks for photosynthesis — are required in large quantities, whether provided by nature or by your watering hose.

Plants also need relatively large amounts of nitrogen, phosphorus, and potassium. These elements are called macronutrients. Secondary nutrients — calcium, magnesium, and sulfur — are required in smaller quantities. And the micronutrients — iron, manganese, copper, boron, molybdenum, chlorine, and zinc — you guessed it, are needed in even smaller amounts.

Macronutrients, secondary nutrients, and micronutrients are mostly absorbed from the soil by plant roots. (These nutrients can also be absorbed by the foliage, but we don't want to get ahead of ourselves.) If any of these nutrients is missing from the soil in sufficient quantities, or is present in a form that the plant can't absorb, fertilizer's in order — or correction of the conditions that make absorbtion difficult.

For plants grown in the ground, most soils already contain enough nutrients needed for healthy growth. Many gardeners find that nitrogen is the only nutrient that they need to apply through fertilizers.

For plants grown in containers, the story changes. If you choose soil mixes sold in bags, fertilizer's already added; if you mix your own soil, you have to incorporate fertilizer as described in Chapter 4. As these nutrients are washed out of the container's soil with frequent watering, you have to replace them.

Why do plants need more nitrogen? Look toward healthy growth. As a key part of plant proteins and chlorophyll, the plant pigment that plays a vital role in photosynthesis, nitrogen is responsible for the green color of plant leaves. Plants that are nitrogen deficient show a yellowing of older leaves first, along with a general slowdown in growth.

Phosphorus and potassium also play important roles in plant growth. Phosphorus is associated with good root growth, plus flower, fruit, and seed production. Potassium is also necessary for healthy roots, disease resistance, and fruiting. Deficiencies in either nutrient are hard to read through symptoms on a plant. Only a soil test can tell for sure; you can buy small soil test kits or have your soil tested through your local cooperative extension service.

Because phosphorus and potassium are less mobile than other nutrients, you can't apply them with watering like you do with nitrogen. Mixing phosphorus and potassium with your soil assures that your roots can absorb the important nutrients.

Translating the Chemistry Listed on Labels

At first glance, a nursery shelf lined with fertilizers is a bewildering sight. But confusion doesn't have to crowd your senses. Among all the colorful bags, bottles, and jars, consistency in labeling can guide you through the jungle of jargon and lead you to the fertilizer that's best for you.

When you buy a commercial fertilizer, the guaranteed analysis is listed on the label with three numbers. These three numbers tell you how much of each of the macronutrients is in the fertilizer. The first number indicates the percentage of nitrogen; the second, the percentage of phosphate; and the third, the percentage of potash, which is chemical mumbo jumbo for potassium. A 10-5-5 fertilizer is 10 percent nitrogen, 5 percent phosphate, and 5 percent potash.

Do the math and you find that a 100-pound bag of 10-5-5 fertilizer contains 10 pounds of nitrogen, 5 pounds of phosphorus, and 5 pounds of potash — a total of 20 pounds of usable nutrients. Although the remaining 80 pounds contain some useful nutrients (also listed on the label), most of the balance is either filler or carrier left over from manufacturing.

A fertilizer's guaranteed analysis is your best shopping guide. But before we dig deeper into the numbers and what they mean, check out some important fertilizer terminology.

First, most fertilizers are sold either in granular or liquid form.

Granular fertilizers

Granular fertilizers are most common. Available in bags or boxes, either partially or completely soluble, granular fertilizers can be scattered over the soil and watered in, or worked into the soil before planting. Completely soluble types are mixed with water and applied when you irrigate. Except for the completely soluble types, granular fertilizers are not ideally suited for feeding container plants. Spreading granules evenly over the top of soil in a pot is difficult — half the container may get more fertilizer than the other half. Because granules take time to dissolve, nutrients may not readily reach plant roots.

Liquid fertilizers

Liquid fertilizers are available in bottles or jugs. On a per nutrient basis, most liquid fertilizers are more expensive than granular ones. Most liquid fertilizers need to be diluted in water before you apply them, but some are ready to use. Liquid fertilizers are applied when you water and can be injected into irrigation systems, which is the reason many professional growers prefer them. Liquids are particularly well-suited for plants grown in containers. Some liquid fertilizers are sold in hose-end applicators, which eliminate the need for mixing.

Fertilizer lingo to know

Before you venture off to ring up your newfound fertilizer knowledge, consider a few more words of wisdom on the language of container plants:

✔ **Complete fertilizers** contain all three macronutrients — nitrogen (N), phosphorus (P), and potassium (K). The term "complete" is linked more to fertilizer industry laws and regulations than to satisfaction of the plant's actual requirements for nutrients.

✔ An **incomplete fertilizer** is missing one or more of the major nutrients, usually the P or the K. Fish emulsion, which usually has a guaranteed analysis of 5-0-0, is an incomplete fertilizer. Incomplete is not necessarily bad. In fact, less is sometimes good enough. Incomplete fertilizers are usually less expensive; if your soil has plenty of P and K, why apply more? Too much can harm your plants.

✔ **Chelated micronutrients** are in a form that allows them to be absorbed into a plant quicker than the more commonly available sulfated forms. If your plants just won't green up (they stay mottled yellow and green, or just plain yellow), no matter how much nitrogen you apply, you probably have a micronutrient deficiency of iron, zinc, or manganese. Chelated micronutrients are the quickest fix, although you may also have a soil pH problem that's preventing the nutrients from being absorbed by the plant (see Chapter 4 for more information on pH).

✔ **Foliar fertilizers** are applied to the leaves of plants rather than to the roots. Amazing — and logical — as it may seem, leaves can absorb nutrients too. Leaves aren't as effective as roots, but they do absorb quickly — so foliar feeding is a good fast feed. Most liquid fertilizers can be used as foliar fertilizers, but make sure that the label instructs you accordingly. Don't apply fertilizers in hot weather because they may burn the leaves.

✔ **Organic fertilizers** derive their nutrients from something that was once alive. Examples are blood meal, fish emulsion, and manure. Usually, organic fertilizers contain significant amounts of only one of the major nutrients; for example, bonemeal contains mostly phosphorus. (The nutrient contents of the most common organic fertilizers are listed in Table 11-1.) Nutrients in organic fertilizers are made available to plant roots after breakdown by soil microorganisms, which usually takes place faster in warm soil. Fish emulsion, a liquid organic fertilizer, is one of the more useful for container plants. Fish emulsion dissolves easily in water and gives good results, but is a bit smelly. Most dry organic fertilizers are best mixed with the soil before you plant. However, they must be used carefully to avoid burning the plants.

- **Slow-release fertilizers** provide nutrients to plants at specific rates under particular conditions. For example, Osmocote fertilizers release nutrients in response to soil moisture. The nutrients inside the tiny beads "osmose" through a resin membrane. Some slow-release, often called timed-release, fertilizers can deliver the benefits of their nutrients for as long as eight months. Slow-release fertilizers are very useful for container plants that otherwise need frequent fertilizing. Be warned: Slow-release fertilizers are very expensive. And when plants are growing quickly, they made need more nitrogen than the slow-release fertilizer can provide. Watch your container plants carefully. If plants grow slowly or are a bit yellowish even on a diet of slow-release fertilizer, give them a boost with an application of regular fertilizer.

- **Specialty fertilizers** are supposedly formulated for specific types of plants. For example, you may find that a fertilizer labeled Flower Food with an analysis of 0-10-10. The logic behind such a fertilizer is that a blooming plant needs more P and K than it does N. That's because the P and K are important in the formation of flowers, and the N promotes leaves. And we want flowers right? Well, not so fast. Remember that we told you how P and K don't move into the soil as well as N does. So you can apply all the P and K that you want and these major nutrients may not get to the roots. Besides, if you are using a good potting mix, there's probably plenty of P and K already.

The truth be told, we think specialty fertilizers are more marketing strategy than high-tech solution — and more expense than can be expected with other fertilizers. If your container plants need nitrogen, and they probably do, then that, and only that, is what you need to apply.

Shopping for Fertilizer Bargains

Now that you're pretty familiar with different types of fertilizers, especially those that offer the ever-important nitrogen, consider a closer look at product labels to find out how they can help make you a better shopper.

Fertilizer prices are all over the place. Premixed liquid fertilizers are among the products that don't cost-compare equally with the amount of nutrients they contain. Fertilizers may be filled with a lot of water, which makes them heavy and more expensive to ship, so they're even pricier. However, premixed varieties are also easy to use on container plants. A simple formula can help you compare the costs of nutrients in different fertilizers.

If a 10-pound bag of fertilizer contains 10 percent nitrogen, it includes 1 pound of what's called actual nitrogen (determined by multiplying the weight of the package by the percentage of nitrogen). By figuring out the actual nitrogen in different packages of fertilizer, you can compare the price of nutrients.

For example, say the 10-pound bag of fertilizer with 10 percent nitrogen costs $5. The price of the one pound of actual nitrogen is $5 (the price divided by the pounds of actual nitrogen). Compare it to a 20-pound bag with 20 percent nitrogen, or 4 pounds of actual nitrogen, costing $10; the cost of the actual nitrogen is $2.50. The larger bag is a better deal. You can not only calculate your way to a bargain, but also treat your plants to a healthy meal — although they probably don't care how much you spend. You can make similar comparison for liquid fertilizer by multiplying the percentage of nitrogen by the ounces of fertilizer in the bottle.

The amount of actual nitrogen in a package of fertilizer also influences application rates. The more actual nitrogen, the less you use with each application. But don't try to figure that out; the manufacturer gives you recommended application rates on the package.

Preparing a Fertilizer Plan

Without doubt, we now really know our fertilizers — the nutrients they contain, the types, and how to shop for them. Next step: fertilizing some container plants.

Plants growing in containers need more water than those growing in the ground. The more you water, the more you flush nutrients from the soil, and the more often you have to fertilize.

You can offset some of this constant loss of nutrients by mixing slow-release fertilizers into the soil mix before planting. But we also recommend the less-food-more-often approach — the best-looking container plants we encounter are on a constant feed program. In other words, they're given a little liquid fertilizer every time, or every other time, that they're watered. Cut the recommended rates on the bottle of fertilizer in half or into quarters, using only about a teaspoon or so of fertilizer per watering. Wait until you see the results. Bloom city!

If frequent feeding poses too much hassle for you, use a liquid or water soluble fertilizer once every week or two. Follow the rates recommended on the label. Your container plants can still respond well.

You can use granular fertilizers on container plants, especially in raised beds. In fact, we often use a lazy person's approach to feeding and just sprinkle a little granular fertilizer in all the pots. Just beware, it's not a very precise technique, and you may burn plants if you put on too much — which we admit to doing more than once.

Discovering Organic Fertilizers

Many people prefer the natural "feel" of organic fertilizers. Truthfully, your plants don't care whether the nutrients they use come from an organic or synthetic form. But organic fertilizers have an advantage in that, besides providing nutrients, they also add bulk to the soil and improve its structure in ways synthetic fertilizers cannot.

However, organic fertilizers are often difficult to handle, their nutrient contents are unpredictable, and the nutrients they do contain are not always immediately available to the plant.

 You can supply all the nutrients that your container plants need by using only organic materials. Dry types are best worked into the soil before you plant. Liquids like fish emulsion are great to apply to growing plants.

Manures from horses, cows, and poultry are among the more commonly used organic sources of nitrogen. The salts in fresh manure can burn plants; be sure that manures age for a while or are completely composted before mixing them with the soil. Many gardeners work manures into raised bed soils in fall and then wait until spring to plant so that the manure has plenty of time to "mellow." Fish emulsion and blood meal are other organic sources of nitrogen.

Bonemeal is a good organic source of phosphorus, but once in the ground, it takes a long time to break down into a form that plants can use. Greensand is an excellent organic source of potassium and also includes many micronutrients.

Table 11-1 lists some common organic fertilizers, their average nutrient analysis, and moderate rates at which they can be applied. Remember that nutrient contents of organic fertilizers can vary greatly. Use less if you have doubts.

Table 11-1	Common Organic Fertilizers	
Organic Fertilizer	*Average Nutrient Analysis*	*Application Rate for 100 Square Feet of Raised Bed*
Blood meal	10-0-0	2 lbs
Bonemeal (steamed)	1-11-0	2 lbs
Cow manure	2-2-2	10 to 15 lbs
Fish emulsion	4-1-1	15 to 20 gallons (1T per gallon)
Greensand	0-0-7	5 lbs
Horse manure	2-1-2	10 to 15 lbs
Poultry manure	4-4-2	5 lbs

Recognizing Too Much of a Good Thing

Overfertilizing can be much worse than not applying enough nutrients. Excess nitrogen, for example, can burn the edges of leaves and even kill a plant. Besides that, if you apply too much, fertilizer can leach into ground water, and then you're a nasty polluter. Always follow label instructions and only apply nutrients that you know are needed — too much of any additive can cause problems with plants and the environment. If you have doubts, have your soil mix tested.

Also, don't apply fertilizer to dry plants or during extremely hot or windy weather, conditions that can cause burn to your container garden.

Chapter 12

When Bad Things Happen: Pests and Diseases

*T*he big, wide, wonderful world of container plants — everything from annuals to trees to cactus — also includes the big, wide, wonderful world of pests and diseases that afflict all this plant diversity.

But fear not, pests usually trouble our container plants less than they bug the same plants in other areas of the garden. The reason is in the way that you grow plants in containers — nearby, up close, right there. In other words, you're more intimate with container plants, and you can keep an eye on them much easier than you're able to do with outlying parts of the garden. Containers are where you are — on the patio, on the porch, on the deck.

If a problem does develop, you usually see it right away and you can take care of it before it gets out of hand. And because container growing makes use of lightweight, sterile soils that start out free of insects and diseases, soil-borne problems are not common.

But when a pest problem develops on your container plants, you want to be able to handle it safely and effectively. And that's what this chapter is all about.

Preventing Pests and Diseases

Many gardeners, especially beginners, are truly surprised at how many pest and disease problems can actually be prevented or avoided. Now, we don't mean prevention through weekly sprays of pesticides that kill any insect or disease organism that approaches within 10 feet of your containers. An annihilator is not the kind of gardener we want you to be.

We want you to take a more well-rounded approach to pest control. And the key to this approach is knowledge. The more that you know about the plants you grow — the pests that prefer them, the types of pest control measures available, and how to protect the diversity of life that occupies your garden, the less likely you are to have to take drastic measures using strong chemicals.

Being a good observer is also important in our approach to pest control. Monitor your plants regularly; look under, over, between, and around the leaves and stems for any signs of infection and infestation.

Don't throw a fit if you see nibblings of a few pests; these pests are food for beneficial predators like lady bugs and lacewings. But if you find masses of crawling insects or rapidly spreading diseases, you need to act fast and take measures to prevent problems from getting out of hand.

Identify any suspicious insect, leaf spot, or growth that you find so that you can determine whether it's a problem. For a start, consult our list of common pests and diseases coming up later in this chapter.

If you need more help, contact a full-service garden center that has a variety of reference books to consult as well as personal experience with local problems. At your nursery or library, ask to see *The Ortho Problem Solver,* a 1,000-page encyclopedia of garden pest problems, each one with a color picture. Also check with a botanical garden or local extension service office; look for the telephone number of your extension office in the telephone book under county listings for cooperative extension or farm advisor.

Smart gardening to prevent pests

If you do the right things for your plants, they're better equipped to fend off insect attacks. Here's a list of common-sense pest prevention measures.

Plant in the right location

Many pests become more troublesome when plants are grown in conditions that are less than ideal. For example, when sun-loving plants are grown in shade, mildew problems often become more severe.

Grow healthy plants

How many times do we need to say it? Healthy plants are less likely to have problems. Start with a good soil mix as recommended in Chapter 4. Water and fertilize regularly so that plants grow strong and more pest-resistant.

Choose resistant plants

If you know a certain disease is common in you area, choose plants that are not susceptible or that resist infection. Some varieties of annuals are resistant to specific diseases. For example, some varieties of snapdragons resist rust, and several varieties of both delphiniums and zinnias resist mildew. Some varieties of roses are more disease-resistant than others, as are many varieties of vegetables.

Encourage and use beneficial insects

Beneficial insects are the good bugs that live in the garden — the insects that feed on the bugs that bother your plants. You probably have a bunch of different kinds in your garden already, but you can also purchase them and release them into your garden. You can also plant flowers that attract beneficial insects. We talk about those later in this chapter.

Keep your garden clean

Simply by cleaning up spent plants and other garden debris, you can eliminate hiding places for many pests.

Know the enemy

The more that you know about specific pests and diseases common to your area — when they occur and how they spread — the more easily you can avoid them. For example, some diseases, like rust, black spot, and botrytis, run rampant on wet foliage. By simply adjusting your watering so that you don't wet the leaves of the plant, or by watering early in the day so plants dry out quickly, you can reduce the occurrence of these diseases.

Encouraging good insects

Gardens typically are populated by huge numbers of different insects, most neither good nor bad. The critters are just hanging out at no expense to the plants. But some insects are definitely beneficial, waging a constant battle with the insects that are bugging our plants.

Good bugs are no fools. They hang out in gardens that offer the most diverse and reliable menu. That's why eliminating every last insect pest from your garden makes no sense — and can be detrimental to your plants.

Our approach to pest control is founded on maximum diversity in the garden. Variety means having some "bad" bugs around all the time. Aphids are like hors d'oeuvres for some many helpful insects, so you always hope to have a few potential meals in your garden. Otherwise, how do you think the good bugs survive?

But accepting the bugs also calls for expecting a little damage once in awhile. So you're really just trying to manage the pests, not nuke them off the face of the earth. You want to keep them at acceptable levels, without letting them get out of control.

That's why being a good observer is so important. Spend time in your garden snooping around. Check your plants frequently, if not daily. If an insect or disease does get out of hand, you want to treat it effectively without disrupting all the other life in the garden, from good bugs all the way to birds. Control measures may be as simple as hand-picking and stepping on snails, or knocking off aphids with a strong jet of water from the hose. You find other physical control measures listed under the individual pests later in this chapter.

To get the good insects to stick around, follow these tips:

✔ Avoid indiscriminate use of broad-spectrum pesticides, which kill the bad bugs *and* the good bugs. If you do spray, use a product that specifically targets the pest that you want to eliminate with minimal effect on beneficial insects.

✔ Maintain a diverse garden with many kinds and sizes of plants. Doing so gives the beneficials places to hide and reproduce. Variety can also provide an alternative food source, because many beneficials like to eat pollen and flower nectar, too. Some plants that attract beneficials include Queen Anne's lace, parsley (especially if you let the flower develop), sweet alyssum, dill, fennel, and yarrow.

✔ If beneficials are not as numerous in your garden as you want, you can buy them from mail-order garden suppliers (we list several in the Appendix). If you know that a particular pest is likely to appear, order in advance. That way you can release the beneficials in time to prevent problems.

Following are some beneficial insects that you can buy to help control pests that trouble annuals:

✔ **Lady beetles:** These are your basic ladybugs. Both the adult and the lizard-like larvae are especially good at feeding on small insects like aphids and thrips. Releasing adults is sometimes not very effective because Mother Nature has preprogrammed them to migrate on down the road, so they leave your garden quickly.

Try preconditioned lady beetles, which have been deprogrammed (you don't want to know how); they're more likely to stick around. And release them just before sundown. That way, they at least spend the night. Release a few thousand of them in spring as soon as you notice the first aphid.

✔ **Green lacewings:** Their voracious larvae feed on aphids, mites, thrips, and various insect eggs. These insects are among the more effective pest control forces. Release them in your garden in late spring, after the danger of frost has passed.

✔ **Parasitic nematodes:** These microscopic worms parasitize many types of soil-dwelling and burrowing insects, including cutworms and grubs of Japanese beetles. Because grubs usually inhabit lawns, you have to apply these worms there, too. Also apply parasitic nematodes to the soil around the base of your plants once in spring.

✔ **Predatory mites:** This type of mite feeds on spider mites and thrips. Add them to your garden in spring as soon as frost danger has passed.

✔ **Trichogramma wasps:** Harmless to humans, these tiny wasps attack moth eggs and butterfly larvae (that is, caterpillars). Release trichogramma when temperatures are above 72°F.

When trouble begins

If friendly bug-eaters don't do the trick, take further action with what we consider our first line of defense against pest outbreaks: pesticides that can be very effective against a certain pest, are pretty safe to use, and have a mild impact on the rest of the garden's life forms.

In general, these products are short-lived after you use them in the garden — that's what makes them so good. However, in order to gain effective control, you often have to use them more frequently than stronger chemicals.

Here are our favorite controls:

✔ **Biological controls:** This method involves pitting one living thing against another. Releasing beneficial insects is one example of biological control, but you can also use bacteria, that while harmless to humans, make insect pests very sick and eventually, very dead.

The most common and useful are forms of *Bacillus thuringiensis,* or Bt, which kills the larvae of moths and butterflies — also known as caterpillars. One type of Bt (sold as milky spore) kills the larvae of Japanese beetles.

✔ **Botanical insecticides:** These insecticides are derived from plants. The following are most useful against the pests of annual flowers:

- **Neem** comes from the tropical tree *Azadirachta indica.* It kills young feeding insects and deters adult insects but is harmless to people and most beneficials. Neem works slowly and is most effective against aphids, thrips, and whitefly, but it also repels Japanese beetles.

  We prefer neem *oil* over neem *extract* (check the product label) because oil is also effective against two common diseases, powdery mildew and rust. Neem oil gets thick when cool, so you need to warm it up before mixing it with water.

  Use either kind of neem before you have a major pest problem. Neem is most effective when applied early in the morning or late in the evening when humidity is high. Reapply after rain.

  Currently, you can buy neem oil only from Green Light Co., Box 17985, San Antonio, TX 78217; 210-494-3481. An 8-ounce container costs about $13, and you need to use 2 tablespoons per gallon of water.

- **Pyrethrins** are derived from the painted daisy, *Chrysanthemum cinerariifolium.* A broad-spectrum insecticide, pyrethrins kill a wide range of insects, both good (spray late in the evening to avoid killing bees) and bad.

  That's the downside. The upside is that this insecticide kills pests like thrips and beetles quickly, and has low toxicity to mammals, which means it's essentially harmless to humans and the environment.

  The terminology can be confusing, however. *Pyrethrum* is the ground-up flower of the daisy. *Pyrethrins* are the insecticide components of the flower. *Pyrethroids,* such as permethrin and resmethrin, are synthetic compounds that resemble pyrethrins but that are more toxic and persistent.

Consequently, we prefer to avoid pyrethroids for home garden use.

- **Rotenone** is derived from the roots of tropical legumes. It breaks down quickly but is more toxic than some commonly used traditional insecticides. Rotenone is a broad-spectrum insecticide, killing beneficials, including bees, and pests alike. Use as a last resort to control various caterpillars, beetles, and thrips.

✔ **Summer oil:** When sprayed on a plant, this highly refined oil smothers pest insects and their eggs. The words "highly refined" mean that the sulfur and other components of the oil that damage the plant are removed. Summer oil is relatively nontoxic and short-lived. Use to control aphids, mites, thrips, and certain caterpillars.

Make sure you do not confuse summer oil with dormant oil. Dormant oil is meant to be applied to leafless trees and shrubs during winter. It is very useful for smothering overwintering pests on roses and fruit trees and is often combined with a fungicide like lime sulfur or fixed copper.

Double-check the product label to make sure that it says it can be used on plants during the growing season. Then follow the mixing instructions carefully. Water the plants before and after applying and don't spray if temperatures are likely to rise above 85°F. When it's that hot, the oil can damage plant leaves.

✔ **Insecticidal soaps:** Derived from the salts of fatty acids, insecticidal soaps kill mostly soft-bodied pests like aphids, spider mites, and whiteflies. Soaps can also be effective against Japanese beetles. They work fast, break down quickly, and are nontoxic to humans. Insecticidal soaps are most effective when mixed with soft water. Soaps sometimes burn tender foliage.

Using synthetic insecticides

You can successfully control most insect problems using the techniques and products we just covered. If, however, a pest really gets out of hand on a prized planting, you may want to use something more serious. Try other control measures before you resort to synthetic pesticides because using them may disrupt the balance of your garden. When you use any pesticide, make sure that you have the pest identified correctly and follow labeled instructions precisely.

Insects That Prey on Container Plants

Here are the most common insect pests that you're likely to find infesting your container plants and the best ways to control them:

Aphids

Aphids are tiny, pear-shaped pests (see Figure 12-1) that come in many colors including black, green, and red. They congregate on new growth and flower buds, sucking plant sap with their needlelike noses. Heavy infestations can cause distorted growth and weakened plants.

WARNING!

Pesticide safety

No matter which pesticides you decide to use, you must use them safely. Even pesticides that have relatively low impact on your garden environment, including several commonly used botanical insecticides, can be toxic to humans and pets.

Always follow instructions on the product label exactly. Doing otherwise is against the law. Both the pest you're trying to control and the plant you're spraying (sometimes plants are listed as groups, such as flowers) must be listed on the label.

Wear gloves when mixing and spraying pesticides. Spray when the winds are calm. Store chemicals in properly labeled containers well out of reach of children (a locked cabinet is best). Dispose of empty containers as described on the label, or contact your local waste disposal company for appropriate disposal sites.

Many plants can be infested including annuals, roses, and many vegetables. Aphids leave behind a sticky sap that may turn black with sooty mold.

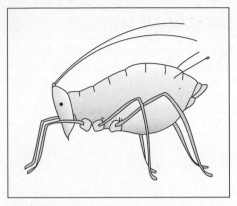

Figure 12-1: An aphid.

Aphids are easy to control. You can knock them off sturdy plants with strong jets of water from a hose, or use insecticidal soap or pyrethrins. The soap also helps wash off the sooty mold (the harmless black gunk that comes with aphids).

If you just wait a week or two, the aphid population boom is followed by a buildup of beneficials, especially lady beetles, and they usually take matters into their own hands before serious damage occurs.

Borers

Several kinds of beetle and caterpillar larvae (they look like small worms and are usually less than an inch long) tunnel into the wood or stems of fruit trees, white birches, dogwoods, shade trees, rhododendrons, and German iris. The boring weakens the plant and makes it more susceptible to disease. The damage can also cut off nutrient flow to the infested limb. Choose varieties that are less susceptible.

For example, try Siberian irises instead of German irises. Keep susceptible plants growing vigorously and watch for signs of borer damage — dead bark, sawdust piles, poor performance. When you find borers, cut off and destroy severely infested limbs. Inject parasitic nematodes into remaining borers holes. You can also use preventive insecticide sprays to kill mating adults or hatching larvae.

Caterpillars and worms

Moth and butterfly larvae are avid eaters and can cause a lot of damage to a variety of plants. Some are hairy caterpillars, others are smooth-skinned and more wormlike. You can hand-pick them to reduce numbers or release trichogramma wasps. But the most effective way to get rid of caterpillars is to spray with Bt. Pyrethrins also work.

Geranium budworms

Geranium budworms are very frustrating pests of geraniums, nicotiana, ageratum, and petunias. The small caterpillars bore into flower buds and eat the flowers before they open, or they just feed on open blooms. The result is no flowers, just leaves.

Great. To confirm the presence of these heartless monsters, look for small holes in geranium blossoms, or the tiny black droppings the caterpillars leave behind. You may also see the worms on the flowers. To control, pick off infested geranium buds and spray with Bt. Pyrethrins, carbaryl, and acephate also work.

Japanese beetles

Japanese beetles can really be troublesome east of the Mississippi River. The ½-inch-long beetles have coppery bodies and metallic green heads. They feed on both flowers and foliage, often skeletonizing leaves. They particularly love zinnias, marigolds, and roses.

Control can be tough. Treating your lawn and garden soil with parasitic nematodes or milky spore (a form of Bt) may reduce the white C-shaped larvae, but more adults may fly in from your neighbor's yard. Floral-scented traps that attract adult beetles are available, but the traps may attract more beetles than you had before. If you try the traps, keep them at least 100 feet from your flowers.

Neem, insecticidal soap, and pyrethrins are effective against adult beetles. Traditional chemicals that may help include carbaryl and acephate. You can also just pick the beetles off your flowers and stomp on them.

Mealybugs

These small sucking insects, most common on houseplants, cover their bodies with a white cottony substance that makes them easy to identify. They usually feed in groups, forming a cottony mass on branches and stems. Wash off small numbers with cotton dipped in rubbing alcohol; for larger infestations, spray with insecticidal soap or neem.

Cutworms

Cutworms are ½-inch-long, grayish caterpillars. They emerge on spring and early summer nights to eat the stems of young seedlings, causing them to fall over like small timbers. They also move onto older plants and feed on leaves and flowers.

To protect seedlings, surround their stems with a barrier that prevents the cutworms from crawling close and feeding. These barriers can be as simple as an empty cardboard toilet paper roll, a Styrofoam cup with the bottom cut out, or a collar made from aluminum foil — just make sure that it encircles the stem completely and is set 1 inch deep in the soil.

You can also trap cutworms by leaving boards around the garden. The worms hide there during the day when you can collect them. Parasitic nematodes are also effective against cutworms.

Scale

Like bumps on plant stems and leaves, these tiny sucking insects cling to plant branches, hiding under an outer shell cover that serves as a shield. These pests suck plant sap and can kill plants if present in large numbers.

Look for sticky, honeylike sap droppings, one clue that scale may be present. Remove and destroy badly infested stems.

Clean off light infestations with a cottony ball soaked in rubbing alcohol. Spray with dormant oil in winter or summer oil during the growing season.

Snails and slugs

Snails and slugs are soft-bodied mollusks that feed on tender leaves and flowers during the cool of the night or during rainy weather. Snails have shells, slugs don't. (A slug is shown in Figure 12-2). Both proliferate in damp areas, hiding under raised containers, boards, or garden debris. To control snails and slugs, you can roam the garden at night with a flashlight and play pick-and-stomp, or you can trap them with saucers of beer with the rim set at ground level. Refill regularly.

Snails and slugs refuse to cross copper, so you can also surround raised beds or individual containers with a thin copper stripping sold in most nurseries or hardware stores. In southern California, you can release decollate snails, which prey on pest snails. Ask your cooperative extension office for information. If all else fails, you may want to put out poison snail bait.

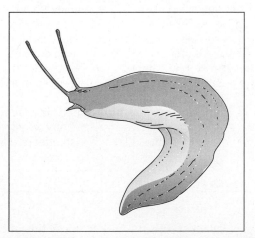

Figure 12-2: A slug.

Spider mites

Spider mites are tiny, spiderlike arachnids that you can barely see without a magnifying glass. One is shown in Figure 12-3. If the population gets big enough, you can see telltale fine webbing beneath the leaves. And as the mites suck plant juices, the leaves become yellowish with silvery stippling or sheen. The plant may even start dropping leaves. Mites are most common in hot, dry summer climates, and on dusty plants. Houseplants, tomatoes, and roses are commonly infested.

A daily bath with a strong jet of water from a hose can help keep infestations down. You can control spider mites with insecticidal soap, which also helps to clean off plant leaves. Summer oil is also effective, as is releasing predatory mites.

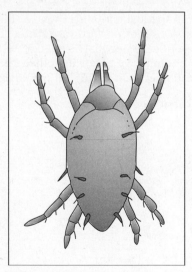

Figure 12-3: A spider mite.

Thrips

Thrips are another almost-invisible troublemaker. They feed on flower petals, causing them to be discolored and the buds to be deformed as they open. They also feed on leaves, causing them to be deformed and giving them a stippled look (which can be distinguished from similar spider mite damage by the small fecal pellets that thrips leave behind). Impatiens, roses, and gladiolus are commonly infested.

Many beneficials feed on thrips, especially lacewings. Insecticidal soaps are also effective against thrips, as are several stronger insecticides, including acephate.

Whiteflies

Whiteflies look like small white gnats (see Figure 12-4), but they suck plant juices and can proliferate in warm climates and greenhouses. They tend to congregate on the undersides of leaves. You can trap whiteflies with yellow sticky traps sold in nurseries. In greenhouses, release Encarsia wasps, which prey on greenhouse whiteflies. Insecticidal soaps, summer oil, and pyrethrins are effective sprays.

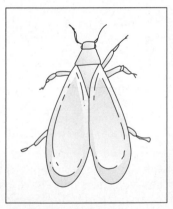

Figure 12-4: A whitefly.

Preventing Diseases

Only a few diseases really do much damage to container-grown plants, and most of those maladies can be prevented or at least reduced in severity with good cultural practices or by planting resistant varieties. If you know a certain disease is a problem on a particular plant in your area, simply grow something else. There are surely many other choices and you may have a good time finding them.

Here are some cultural practices that can help avoid plant diseases. Some of these we mentioned earlier, but they're worth repeating here:

- **Remove infected plants.** As soon as you notice a plant with a problem, give it the yank. Even picking off infected leaves helps prevent a disease from spreading.

- **Avoid overhead watering.** Or at least water early in the morning so that plants have a chance to dry out before nightfall. Using drip irrigation or watering in furrows also helps keep foliage dry. Overhead watering can cause more problems than just encouraging foliage disease organisms — it can ruin many flowers, causing them to be washed out or look like they somehow melted. Bloom damage often happens with petunias and geraniums.

- **Space plants properly.** Planting too close reduces air circulation between plants — a condition that invites disease. Unfortunately, planting close together is often the way to achieve the best look with container plantings like annuals. Just be aware that diseases are more common under these conditions, and keep your eyes open for developing problems.

- **Keep your garden clean and tidy.** Many diseases spread on plant debris, so rake up fallen leaves and remove dead plants. Keep the spaces under containers clean. Removing diseased leaves can slow the spread of some organisms.

- **Provide drainage.** Make sure that your pots can drain properly. You know that your pots must have holes in the bottom so that water can drain out. But frequent checks also allow you to be sure that the openings aren't clogged with roots. And if you have a catch pan under your pots, make sure that it isn't constantly full of water, preventing water from draining out of the pot. Believe this — constantly soggy soil is a big contributor to root-rot diseases.

- **Use fresh soil mix.** Don't replant in the same soil mix, especially if you're growing plants that may be susceptible to diseases. Dump out the old, refill with the new.

Seven Dastardly Diseases

Here are some tips on the prevention, identification, and — if possible — treatment of some common plant diseases.

Black spot

Like its name suggests, this fungus causes black spots on leaves and stems. Black spot is most troublesome on roses, but it can also attack various fruiting plants. On roses, the edges of the spots are fringed and the tissue around the spots often turns yellow. In bad infections, the plant may drop all its leaves. The disease is most common in warm, humid climates with frequent summer rain.

The best advice to prevent black spot (besides planting disease-resistant varieties) is to clean up your winter prunings — the most common source of reinfection — and use a dormant spray that includes lime sulfur. Also, avoid overhead watering or water early in the morning so that leaves can dry out quickly. The baking soda-summer oil combination mentioned under "Powdery mildew" later in this chapter also provides some control, as does neem oil.

WARNING!

Our outlook on fungicides

Chemical fungicides are one of the nastier bunch of pesticides. If we can get away with it, we prefer not to use them. If, however, you develop a really stubborn disease in a prized planting, you may have no choice. But before you spray, make sure you have the disease properly identified. Enlist the help from a local nurserymen or cooperative extension specialist to confirm your suspicions. Then use a product specifically labeled for the disease you're trying to cure. Follow the label instructions exactly.

Botrytis blight

Also called gray mold, this fungal disease overwinters on plant debris and is common on strawberries, petunias, and other flowers. The blight is most notable as gray fuzz forming on old flowers and fruit, turning them to moldy mush, but it can also discolor or spot foliage. It's most troublesome on older plant parts and in cool, humid weather. Make sure that plants are properly spaced and avoid overhead watering. Remove and destroy any infected plant parts.

Damping off

This fungus attacks the base of seedling stems, causing them to wilt and fall over. The best way to prevent the disease is to plant seeds in sterile potting soil and avoid over-watering. To prevent recurring problems after an infestation, clean containers well and fill your pots with fresh soil. If the disease gains a foothold, it's hard to stop.

Powdery mildew

This fungus coats leaves and flowers with a white powder. The mildew is most common when days are warm but nights are cool, and is particularly troublesome on zinnias, dahlias, begonias, roses, squash, melons, and peas. Control is difficult, but there are resistant varieties. The disease also becomes less of a problem as the weather changes, so if you keep young plants growing vigorously, they may grow out of susceptibility. Neem oil may also help.

Near the end of the season, you may want to pull annual plants out early and start with something new. Rose growers have some success using a mixture of 1 tablespoon of summer oil and 1 or 2 teaspoons of baking soda in a gallon of water; you have to use the mix often to protect new foliage. Another rose grower's technique: spraying plants with antitranspirants. These materials, sold with names like Cloud Cover or Wiltpruf, coat leaves with a thin waxy film that seems to prevent the mildew from getting established — worth a try.

Root rots

A number of soilborne fungi cause plants to basically do the same thing — suddenly wilt and die, whether or not the soil is moist. Vinca is notorious for checking out like this. The best way to prevent root rot is to use sterile soil, make sure that your pots drain properly, and avoid overwatering — let the soil dry partially between irrigations. Otherwise, all you can do is remove the dead plants. Few other control measures are effective.

Rust

This fungal disease is easy to identify: It forms rusty pustules on the undersides of plant leaves. Gradually the upper sides of the leaves turn yellow and the whole plant begins to decline. Snapdragons, roses, and hollyhocks are common hosts. To avoid rust, plant resistant varieties. Also, space plants for good air circulation, keep the garden clean, and avoid overhead watering. Destroy infected plants.

Salt burn

Salt burn isn't actually a disease caused by a living organism, but rather a malady caused by excess salts building up in the soil. It's common in windy areas, where irrigation water is high in salts, or when plants are over-fertilized. Japanese maples are particularly sensitive to salt burn. The symptoms are pretty easy to recognize — leaf edges become dry and crispy — much like what happens when a plant becomes too dry.

If the condition worsens, the whole leaf may dry up and drop, and tips of branches may die. Similar symptoms occur if you let a plant get too dry. The solution is to water the container heavily and leach the salts out of the soil. To get all the salts out, you may have to fill the pot with water more than six or seven times. As long as the container has good drainage, you really can't overdo it. You may also want to reduce your fertilizing or move the pot to an area that's protected from wind.

Chapter 13

Ten Container Plants for Spring, Summer, Fall, and Winter

In This Chapter

▶ For every season: plants year-round

Depending on your climate, you can enjoy the company of appealing container plants at almost any time of year. (Of course, your options are limited in winter in cold climates.)

Here are just a few of many annuals, perennials, bulbs, and permanent plants that perform particularly well at various seasons:

Spring

- Azalea
- Calendula
- Columbine
- Daffodil
- Felicia
- Iceland poppy
- Primrose

- Rose
- Snapdragon
- Tulip

Summer

- Geranium
- Dahlia
- Daylily
- Fuchsia
- Hibiscus
- Impatien
- Lobelia
- Marigold
- Petunia
- Zinnia

Fall

- Aster
- Chrysanthemum
- Dwarf pomegranate
- Flowering cabbage
- Heavenly bamboo
- Japanese maple
- Pansy
- Rose
- Sasanqua camellia
- Sweet olive *(Osmanthus fragrans)*

Winter

- Camellia
- Cyclamen
- Holly
- Pyracantha
- Primrose

Living Christmas Trees

- Colorado spruce
- Dwarf Alberta spruce
- Noble fir
- Scotch pine
- White fir

Index

• E •

Early Cal Wonder, sweet pepper, 102
Early Cascade, tomato variety, 103
east exposures, partial shade, 21
Easter Egg, radish variety, 102
Echeveria, container succulent, 116
Echinocatus grusonii (golden barrel cactus), 115
Echinocereus viridiflorus (hedgehog cactus), 115
Echinopis (sea urchin), 115
education, pest/disease, 144
eggplants, 100–101
elevation, advantages, 31–32
Encarsia wasps, whitefly control, 155
English ivy, container, 32
English laurel, privacy screens, 13
English lavender, container, 32
English primrose (*Primula polyantha*), 93
Epiphyllum (orchid cactus), 115
erigeron, 94
euryops, 91
Euryops pectinatus, 91
evaporation, wood container, 25
evergreens, 65, 82
Excelsior, foxglove variety, 91

• F •

Fafard Mixes, soil mix, 42
fall season, suggestions, 162
Fanfare, cucumber variety, 100
Fantasy, petunia strain, 78
Felicia (blue marguerite), 89
fennel, beneficial insect, 145
fern (azalea) pots, size/shape, 30
ferns, 13, 21, 30, 40
fertilizers, 37, 43, 60, 89, 74–75, 86, 97, 113, 131–140
fir bark, soil mix, 42, 43

fish emulsion, 135, 138–139
fleicia, spring season, 161
flexibility, container gardening, 22
floral-scented traps, 151
flowering cabbage, fall season, 162
foliage, sun/shade reaction, 21–22
foliar fertilizers, 135
Fordhook Giant, Swiss chard, 103
formal style, 11, 13
foxglove (*Digitalis*), 91
Foxy, foxglove variety, 91
freezes, 70, 124
French marigolds, sun location, 77
front entrance, topiary ivy balls, 13
front steps, white marguerites, 13
frost, annual reaction to, 70
fruit trees, 52, 150–151
fuchsia, 16, 162
fungicides, cautions/concerns, 157

• G •

Gaillardia (blanketflower), 89
garden cleanliness, 143, 156
garden diversity, 145
garden soils, 38–42
gazania, 94
general purpose mix, 44
genetics, watering factor, 120
geranium budworms, 151
geraniums, 32, 40, 77, 82, 151, 162
Gerbera (Transvaal daisy), 78–79
German iris, 150–151
germinating mix, when to use, 44
gladiolus, thrips, 155
glazed clay containers, 25–26
glazed pots, annual suggestions, 72
globe, basil variety, 105
gloriosa, container suggestions, 72
gloves, 56, 110
Gloxiniiflora, foxglove variety, 91
Gold Rush, squash variety, 102
golden barrel cactus (*Echinocatus grusonii*), 13, 32, 115
golden, sage variety, 106

BUSINESS, CAREERS & PERSONAL FINANCE

0-7645-9847-3   0-7645-2431-3

Also available:
- Business Plans Kit For Dummies
  0-7645-9794-9
- Economics For Dummies
  0-7645-5726-2
- Grant Writing For Dummies
  0-7645-8416-2
- Home Buying For Dummies
  0-7645-5331-3
- Managing For Dummies
  0-7645-1771-6
- Marketing For Dummies
  0-7645-5600-2
- Personal Finance For Dummies
  0-7645-2590-5*

- Resumes For Dummies
  0-7645-5471-9
- Selling For Dummies
  0-7645-5363-1
- Six Sigma For Dummies
  0-7645-6798-5
- Small Business Kit For Dummies
  0-7645-5984-2
- Starting an eBay Business For Dummies
  0-7645-6924-4
- Your Dream Career For Dummies
  0-7645-9795-7

HOME & BUSINESS COMPUTER BASICS

0-7645-8958-X   0-7645-7326-8

Also available:
- Buying a Computer For Dummies
  0-7645-9818-X
- Cleaning Windows XP For Dummies
  0-7645-7549-X
- Excel 2003 All-in-One Desk Reference For Dummies
  0-7645-3758-X
- Excel Formulas and Functions For Dummies
  0-7645-7556-2
- Mac OS X Tiger For Dummies
  0-7645-7675-5

- Office 2003 All-in-One Desk Reference For Dummies
  0-7645-3883-7
- QuickBooks All-in-One Desk Reference For Dummies
  0-7645-7662-3
- Quicken 2006 For Dummies
  0-7645-9658-6
- RFID For Dummies
  0-7645-7910-X
- Salesforce.com For Dummies
  0-7645-7921-5
- Upgrading and Fixing Laptops For Dummies
  0-7645-8959-8
- Word 2003 For Dummies
  0-7645-3982-5

FOOD, HOME, GARDEN, HOBBIES, MUSIC & PETS

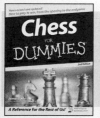

0-7645-8404-9   0-7645-9904-6

Also available:
- Candy Making For Dummies
  0-7645-9734-5
- Card Games For Dummies
  0-7645-9910-0
- Crocheting For Dummies
  0-7645-4151-X
- Dog Training For Dummies
  0-7645-8418-9
- Healthy Carb Cookbook For Dummies
  0-7645-8476-6
- Home Maintenance For Dummies
  0-7645-5215-5

- Horses For Dummies
  0-7645-9797-3
- Jewelry Making & Beading For Dummies
  0-7645-2571-9
- Orchids For Dummies
  0-7645-6759-4
- Puppies For Dummies
  0-7645-5255-4
- Rock Guitar For Dummies
  0-7645-5356-9
- Sewing For Dummies
  0-7645-6847-7
- Singing For Dummies
  0-7645-2475-5

INTERNET & DIGITAL MEDIA

0-7645-9802-3   0-7645-5654-1

Also available:
- BitTorrent For Dummies
  0-7645-9981-X
- Blogging For Dummies
  0-471-77084-1
- Digital SLR Cameras and Photography For Dummies
  0-7645-9803-1
- Digital Video For Dummies
  0-471-78278-5
- Firefox For Dummies
  0-471-74899-4
- Home Recording For Musicians
  0-7645-8884-2

- iPods & iTunes For Dummies
  0-471-74739-4
- Google Search & Rescue For Dummies
  0-7645-9930-5
- The Internet For Dummies
  0-7645-8996-2
- Podcasting For Dummies
  0-471-74898-6
- Search Engine Optimization For Dummies
  0-7645-6758-6
- VoIP For Dummies
  0-7645-8843-5

SPORTS, FITNESS, PARENTING, RELIGION & SPIRITUALITY

0-471-76871-5   0-7645-7841-3

Also available:

- Catholicism For Dummies
  0-7645-5391-7
- Exercise Balls For Dummies
  0-7645-5623-1
- Fitness For Dummies
  0-7645-7851-0
- Football For Dummies
  0-7645-3936-1
- Judaism For Dummies
  0-7645-5299-6
- Potty Training For Dummies
  0-7645-5417-4
- Buddhism For Dummies
  0-7645-5359-3

- Pregnancy For Dummies
  0-7645-4483-7 †
- Ten Minute Tone-Ups
  For Dummies
  0-7645-7207-5
- NASCAR For Dummies
  0-7645-7681-X
- Religion For Dummies
  0-7645-5264-3
- Soccer For Dummies
  0-7645-5229-5
- Women in the Bible
  For Dummies
  0-7645-8475-8

TRAVEL

0-7645-7749-2   0-7645-6945-7

Also available:

- Alaska For Dummies
  0-7645-7746-8
- Cruise Vacations For Dummies
  0-7645-6941-4
- England For Dummies
  0-7645-4276-1
- Europe For Dummies
  0-7645-7529-5
- Germany For Dummies
  0-7645-7823-5
- Hawaii For Dummies
  0-7645-7402-7

- Italy For Dummies
  0-7645-7386-1
- Las Vegas For Dummies
  0-7645-7382-9
- London For Dummies
  0-7645-4277-X
- Paris For Dummies
  0-7645-7630-5
- RV Vacations For Dummies
  0-7645-4442-X
- Walt Disney World & Orlando
  For Dummies
  0-7645-9660-8

GRAPHICS, DESIGN & WEB DEVELOPMENT

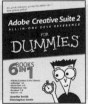

0-7645-8815-X   0-7645-9571-7

Also available:

- 3D Game Animation For
  Dummies
  0-7645-8789-7
- AutoCAD 2006 For Dummies
  0-7645-8925-3
- Building a Web Site For
  Dummies
  0-7645-7144-3
- Creating Web Pages All-in-
  One Desk Reference For
  Dummies
  0-7645-4345-8
- Dreamweaver 8 For Dummies
  0-7645-9649-7
- InDesign CS2 For Dummies
  0-7645-9572-5

- Macromedia Flash 8
  For Dummies
  0-7645-9691-8
- Photoshop CS2 and Digital
  Photography For Dummies
  0-7645-9580-6
- Photoshop Elements 4
  For Dummies
  0-471-77483-9
- Syndicating Web Sites with
  RSS Feeds For Dummies
  0-7645-8848-6
- Yahoo! SiteBuilder
  For Dummies
  0-7645-9800-7

NETWORKING, SECURITY, PROGRAMMING & DATABASES

0-7645-7728-X   0-471-74940-0

Also available:

- Access 2003 All-in-One Desk
  Reference For Dummies
  0-7645-3988-4
- ASP.NET 2 For Dummies
  0-7645-7907-X
- C# 2005 For Dummies
  0-7645-9704-3
- Excel VBA Programming
  For Dummies
  0-7645-7412-4
- Hacking For Dummies
  0-7645-5784-X
- Hacking Wireless Networks
  For Dummies
  0-7645-9730-2

- Microsoft SQL Server 2005
  For Dummies
  0-7645-7755-7
- Networking All-in-One Desk
  Reference For Dummies
  0-7645-9939-9
- Preventing Identity Theft
  For Dummies
  0-7645-7336-5
- Telecom For Dummies
  0-471-77085-X
- Visual Studio 2005 All-in-One
  Desk Reference For Dummies
  0-7645-9775-2
- XML For Dummies
  0-7645-8845-1

Portable Gardening Guides

Each book includes
8 pages of full-color
garden photos!

Notes